ISBN 0-87201-472-X

51295

D1208771

Camper's Guide to
MINNESOTA
Parks, Lakes, Forests, and Trails
Where to Go and How to Get There

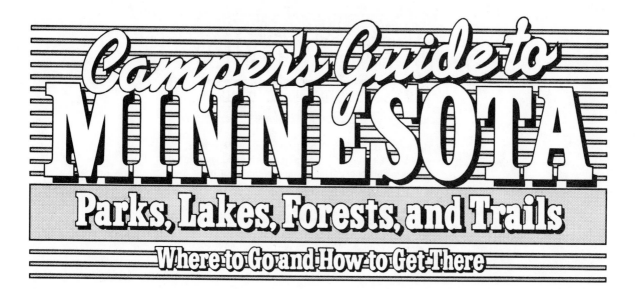

Camper's Guide to MINNESOTA

Parks, Lakes, Forests, and Trails

Where to Go and How to Get There

Mickey Little

Gulf Publishing Company

Camper's Guide to MINNESOTA
Parks, Lakes, Forests, and Trails
Where to Go and How to Get There

Library of Congress Cataloging-in-Publication Data
Little, Mildred J.
    Camper's guide to Minnesota parks, lakes, forests,
and trails
    Mickey Little.
    p. cm.
    Includes index.
    ISBN 0-87201-472-X
    1. Camp sites, facilities, etc.—Minnesota—Directories.
    2. Minnesota—Description and travel—1981—Guide-books.
    I. Title.
    GV191.42.M6L58   1989   89-1793
    647′.94776—dc19   CIP

Capital: St. Paul
Statehood: 1858 (32nd state)
Area: 84,068 square miles; ranks 12th
Population: 4 million +
Motto/Name: The North Star State
Nickname: Land of 10,000 Lakes
State Flower: Pink and White Lady Slipper

State Gemstone: Lake Superior Agate
State Bird: Common Loon
State Tree: Red or Norway Pine
State Fungus: Morel Mushroom
State Grain: Wild Rice
State Fish: Walleye

Also of Interest—

Camper's Guide to Texas Parks, Lakes, and
Forests/Second Edition
Camper's Guide to Florida Parks, Trails,
Rivers, and Beaches
Camper's Guide to California Parks, Lakes,
Forests, and Beaches
Volume 1: Northern California
Volume 2: Southern California
Camper's Guide to Outdoor Cooking
Mariner's Atlas: Lake Michigan

Contents

Region 3, 104

*I went to the woods because I wished to live deliber-
ately, to front only the essential facts of life, and see
if I could not learn what it had to teach, and not,
when I came to die, discover that I had not lived.*

—Henry David Thoreau

Acknowledgments

I am indebted to and wish to thank the following agencies for information—in the form of maps, brochures, telephone conversations, and personal interviews—without which this book would not have been possible:

Chippewa National Forest
Forest Service, U.S. Department of Agriculture
Minnesota Department of Natural Resources
   Bureau of Information and Education
   Division of Forestry
   Division of Parks and Recreation
   Information Center
   Trails and Waterways Unit
Minnesota Department of Transportation
Minnesota Office of Tourism
National Park Service, U.S. Department of the
   Interior
St. Croix National Scenic Riverway
Superior Hiking Trail Association
Superior National Forest
U.S. Army Corps of Engineers, St. Paul District
Voyageurs National Park

While every effort has been made to ensure the accuracy of the information in this guide, neither I nor the publisher assume liability arising from the use of this material. Park facilities and policies are subject to change, so verify the accuracy of important details before beginning a trip.

Mickey Little

The St. Croix River was designated by the U.S. Congress as the nation's first Wild and Scenic River (page 117).

Photo Credits

The Minnesota Department of Natural Resources provided the photos on pages 1, 17, 21, 33, 35, 36, 47, 48, 56, 61, 63, 68, 71, 83, and 132. All other photos are by the author unless credited otherwise.

Introduction

Minnesota—the state's name comes from a Sioux Indian word meaning "sky-tinted water." How appropriate, since Minnesota is second only to Alaska in the amount of water contained within a state's boundary. Minnesota's license plates boast of being the "land of 10,000 lakes," but the truth is that the number of lakes larger than 10 acres is probably closer to 12,000. These lakes are the result of glaciers that blanketed most of the state some 100,000 years ago. Rock and soil were scooped out from the northern and central regions, and when the climate warmed again, the melting ice filled these depressions with water. Lake Superior is a particularly impressive example of the glacier's handiwork.

Minnesota offers a rich variety of landscapes and climates. The park system is one of the best in the nation with 61 state parks having camping facilities. In addition, there are 49 campgrounds in the 2 national forests, 6 recreation areas at lakes administered by the U.S. Army Corps of Engineers, and over 50 recreation areas with campgrounds in various state forests. What better way is there to really see and enjoy the Minnesota outdoors than by camping?

The purpose of this *Camper's Guide* is to suggest places to go and provide directions to get there. You will discover information about the popular, well-known campgrounds as well as the lesser used camping areas. The public campgrounds presented in this guide, provided and operated by state and federal agencies, afford varied options for outdoor recreation. You can fish, boat, canoe, backpack, swim, sail, picnic, bicycle, horseback ride, water ski, or walk along a nature trail. In season, you can also cross-country ski, snow shoe, ice fish, or snowmobile. You can pursue your favorite hobby as a bird watcher, photographer, botanist, geologist, or naturalist. You may choose to rough it at a primitive campsite or to enjoy all of the comforts of home in a recreational vehicle. You can spend a day, a weekend, or an entire vacation doing what you like best, no matter how active, or inactive.

Let's look more closely at the state of Minnesota to see what it has to offer the camping enthusiast. Lying near the geographic center of North America, Minnesota is the northern-most point of the continental United States. It has a width of 348 miles, a length of 406 miles, and is the twelfth largest state in the nation. The major river systems include the Mississippi, Minnesota, and Red River of the North. No water flows into the state, but water flows from Minnesota in three directions—Hudson Bay, Atlantic Ocean, and the Gulf of Mexico. In the north-central part of the state, at Itasca State Park, the Mississippi River begins its 2,552-mile journey to the Gulf of Mexico. These headwaters of the Mississippi were discovered in 1832 by Henry Schoolcraft and his expedition.

Minnesota offers a great variety of outdoor recreational opportunities because it is situated at ecological crossroads for three regions—the western plains and prairies, the northern coniferous forest, and the eastern hardwood forest. Remnants of the once-great prairie with its tall, waving grasses, as well as isolated wooded areas and tree-lined rivers are found in the plains area. This area covers most of the southwestern quarter of the state and the northwestern strip along the Red River Valley border.

The north-central and northeastern areas of Minnesota are very wooded, with pine or pine/hardwood mixed forests, dotted with thousands of lakes. In the northeast along Lake Superior, the terrain is gently rolling with small-scale mountains. Eagle

These wise 'ole owls agree on one thing . . . you'll love camping in Minnesota—the land of 10,000 lakes!

Mountain, northwest of Grand Marais on the North Shore, is the highest point in Minnesota at 2,301 feet above sea level.

In the southeastern quarter of the state, along the Mississippi River valley, is an area of rounded bluffs, valleys bordering meandering streams, and sheer limestone cliffs. This area was once covered by a great hardwood forest, and remnants of those woods still remain in the Richard J. Dorer Memorial Hardwood State Forest and several state parks.

Minnesota's climate is characterized by four distinct seasons, although many natives declare there are only two seasons. The average first fall freeze is October 13 and the average last spring freeze is April 30. The cool summer nights of the northern wooded lake region are a vacationer's dream. The mean summer temperature is 64°F in the north and 70°F in the south. The winters are cold and generally snowy, since the state is dominated by northwesterly winds bringing polar air. The mean winter temperature is 4°F in the north and 14°F in the south.

The state is a water playground for fishing, sailing, canoeing, houseboating, and water skiing. In fact, there is one boat for every seven Minnesotans. These facts are not too surprising when one realizes that the total distance of rivers and streams is 25,000 miles; the total distance of lake and river shoreline is 90,000 miles; and there are 2.6 million acres of boating waters and 3,550 miles of canoeing waters.

The 451-square-mile Red Lake is the largest lake within the state's border. Other major lakes, in order of size, include Lake Superior, Lake of the Woods, Mille Lacs Lake, Leech Lake, Rainy Lake, and Lake Winnibigoshish. Even the cold, snowy winter doesn't stop action on the lakes; snowmobile trails criss-cross from shore to shore and villages of ice fishing houses appear. The ice house population approaches 5,000 people at peak times at Lake Mille Lacs, known as the ice fishing capital of the world.

With all of the water in Minnesota, it's not surprising that the state should have a wide variety of waterfalls and cascades. The major waterfalls are: Big Falls on the Pigeon River on the Canadian border, Caribou Falls on the Caribou River, Gooseberry Falls at Gooseberry Falls State Park, High Falls on the Baptism River at Tettegouche State Park, Manitou Falls at George H. Crosby-Manitou State Park, Minnehaha Falls on Minnehaha Creek, and Minneopa Falls at Minneopa State Park. Other beautiful waterfalls may be viewed at Cascade River State Park, Judge C. R. Magney State Park, and Temperance River State Park—all on Lake Su-

Located along the rocky shoreline of Lake Superior, this is one of five magnificent waterfalls that highlight Gooseberry Falls State Park (page 75).

perior's North Shore. Vermillion Falls, at Crane Lake Inlet, is in a remote setting just outside the southeast corner of Voyageurs National Park.

Lakes are the core of the newest national park in the country—Voyageurs, on the Canadian border—and the Boundary Waters Canoe Area. Voyageurs National Park can be explored by canoe or houseboat; the Boundary Waters by canoe. Over one million acres in size, the Boundary Waters Canoe Area Wilderness extends nearly 150 miles along the Canadian border adjacent to Quetico Provincial Park. It is the nation's only designated canoe wilderness.

When the first explorers came to what is now Minnesota in the 17th century, it was an uneasy battleground of two Indian tribes: the Dakota (Sioux) and the Ojibwa (Chippewa). Today there are 11 Indian reservations. Two national monuments celebrate the rich Indian heritage of the state. Grand Portage National Monument at the northeast tip of Minnesota near Canada was the first non-Indian settlement in the area. The monument is a replica of the original Northwest Fur Company Trading outpost that recalls the Indian heritage and voyageur explorations of yesteryear. Pipestone National Monument in the southwest preserves the quarries of the red stone found in this area, which has been used for centuries in making Indian peacepipes.

Visitors from other states who drive to Minnesota should be aware of the fact that there are nine Highway Travel Information Centers located on major highways entering the state. They are open from 8:00 a.m. to 5:00 p.m. (except some holidays) and give up-to-date information, brochures, guides, and maps to visitors. The centers are located at the following sites:

From Iowa; northbound lane of I-35 at Iowa border (just south of Albert Lea)

From South Dakota: I-90 at South Dakota border (east of Sioux Falls)

From North Dakota: I-94 at North Dakota border (east of Fargo); US 2, 10 miles east of North Dakota's border and Grand Forks (open May-October)

From Canada: US 53 in downtown International Falls

Near Duluth: I-35 at junction of US 2 (when approaching Duluth from the southwest); US 53 at Anchor Lake (approximately 45 miles north of Duluth and just south of Eveleth)

From Wisconsin: I-94 at Wisconsin border (west of the St. Croix River); I-90 at Wisconsin border (west of LaCrosse and west of the Mississippi River)

Prior to a trip, a map and other information may be obtained from the Minnesota Office of Tourism. Their address is:

Minnesota Tourist Information Center
375 Jackson St., 250 Skyway
St. Paul, MN 55101
(612) 296-5029
Toll free inside Minnesota 1-800-652-9747
Toll free outside minnesota 1-800-383-1461

There are rules and regulations encountered at all public campgrounds, whether administered by a state or national agency. Please remember that policies, fees, regulations, and available facilities change from time to time. It's easy for campers to stay informed; merely, by requesting updated information and by reading the materials posted or distributed at the parks they visit.

HOW TO USE THE CAMPER'S GUIDE

The state is divided into three geographic regions, and the parks, lakes, and forests within each region are arranged alphabetically and are cross-listed by name and city in the index. The first page of each region locates the park, lake or forest on the map and gives the page number(s) where you can find more detailed information and maps of that specific area.

All the information in this *Camper's Guide* has been supplied by the respective operating agency, either through literature distributed by them, through verbal communication, or through secondary sources deemed reliable. The information presented is basic—it tells you how to get there, cites outstanding features of the area, and lists the facilities and the recreational activities available. Mailing addresses and telephone numbers are given in case you want additional information prior to your trip. For some parks, it's a good idea to confirm weather and road conditions before heading out.

The maps showing the location of facilities within a park or campground should be of considerable help. These maps are usually available to you at the park headquarters but they can also aid you in planning a trip to an unfamiliar park. Those of you who have attempted to meet up with friends at a predetermined spot at a large campground can readily appreciate the value of having such a map. Most parks are easily found with the help of a good road map, but vicinity maps have been included in some

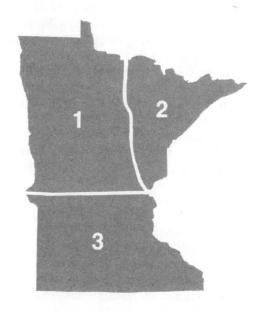

instances. Signs along the way can also be relied upon after you reach the general vicinity of a park. As you travel from one county to another, be aware of the fact that the county road (abreviated CR) numbers change. For example, without your realizing that you crossed the county "line," Cottonwood CR 13 becomes Murray CR 6 as you travel west.

Because each ranger district within a national forest operates somewhat independently of the national forest as a whole, distributes its own materials, and in many ways has its own "personality" because of terrain, recreational opportunities, etc., information on each national forest is arranged by ranger districts. Visitors who wish to camp off-the-beaten-path should certainly purchase the official national forest map because even the best road map often does not show the many back roads in the forest.

The facilities at a campground are always changing, but a change in status usually means the addition of a service rather than a discontinuation. In other words, a camper often finds better and more facilities than those listed in the latest brochure.

The average camper usually doesn't need help deciding what activities to engage in. Obviously, water-related sports are the most popular activities at a lake or river setting. Other possible activities have been listed to indicate the availability of interpretive trails, hiking trails, horseback trails, cross-country ski trails, snowmobile trails, boat ramps, etc. In many parks, interpretive programs, including nature walks, guided tours, and campfire talks, are conducted by park personnel.

May this *Camper's Guide* serve you well in the years ahead, whether you are a beginner or a seasoned camper. Take time to camp, to canoe, to use the trails, to become truly acquainted with nature . . . and with yourself, your family and your friends! Don't put off until tomorrow what can be enjoyed today!

STATE PARKS

Minnesota's state parks are located, virtually, over the entire state: along the borders of Wisconsin, Iowa, South Dakota, North Dakota, Canada, the shoreline of Lake Superior, and everywhere in between. They range in size from the 34,073-acre St. Croix State Park to the 118-acre Franz Jevne State Park. Since 1891, when Itasca became Minnesota's first state park, the number grew to 64. Recently, Little Elbow Lake State Park reverted to the White Earth Indian Reservation, so 63 parks remain in the system. Only two parks, Fort Snelling and Soudan Underground Mine, do not having camping accommodations. The 61 state parks that have camping facilities, whether they be drive-in, walk-in, backpack, or canoe campsites, receive major emphasis in this *Camper's Guide*.

How about an exposure to some state park trivia? Granted, the word "trivia" means unimportant matters, according to *Webster's Dictionary*, but when all is said and done, individual facts take on real meaning when viewed as a whole. After you consider the following facts, gleaned from the chart in the Department of Natural Resources' (DNR) *Guide to Minnesota State Parks*, you will readily agree that the state parks in Minnesota are outstanding in what they have to offer—

▲ With regard to campsites: 57 parks have drive-in sites; 12 parks have walk-in sites; 15 parks have backpack sites; and 16 parks have canoe campsites.

▲ The total number of individual campsites in the above four categories is 4,079.

▲ 27 parks have electrical hook-ups available.

▲ 36 parks have trailer dumping stations.

▲ 46 parks have shower facilities.

▲ All but 9 parks have some form of group campgrounds.

▲ All state parks have picnic areas.

▲ 43 parks have one or more shelters, either open or closed.

▲ 32 parks have swimming facilities.

▲ 57 of the parks have fishing opportunities, either stream, river, or lake.

▲ 41 parks provide boat access, either drive-in or carry.

This couple is dwarfed by the dolomite cliffs at Whitewater State Park (page 136). Located in the blufflands of southeastern Minnesota, the group center at this park is winterized and open year-round.

- ▲ 27 state parks conduct interpretive programs throughout the summer, ranging from guided walks, campfire talks, natural craft programs, and guest speakers.
- ▲ 8 parks offer interpretive services throughout the year.
- ▲ All but 3 of the parks are accessible during the winter; exceptions are Franz Jevne, Monson Lake, and Schoolcraft.
- ▲ 25 parks have warming houses for winter activities.
- ▲ Gooseberry Falls and Wild River state parks have heated shower and toilet buildings in the winter; others have vault toilets in the winter.
- ▲ Most of the parks can accommodate those with handicaps.
- ▲ With regard to trails at all 63 state parks: all of the parks have foot trails; 27 parks have self-guided trails; 18 parks have horse trails; 20 parks have bike trails; 57 parks have cross-country ski trails; and 40 parks have snowmobile trails.
- ▲ The total number of miles of trails in the above list is 2,390!

That completes the list of trivia facts. Wouldn't you agree that the state parks of Minnesota have something for everyone?

Each year various parks will upgrade and/or add facilities and services. To keep abreast of these changes, obtain the latest copy of the *Guide to Minnesota State Parks* brochure, as well as the individual brochure/trail map on the parks that you plan to visit. These are available free through individual parks or from the DNR Information Center.

Campsite Reservation Procedure

Most state parks accept telephone and walk-in reservations for any day of the year. Reservations may be made Monday through Friday, 8:00 a.m. to 4:00 p.m. up to 15 days prior to your arrival. A $3.00 nonrefundable fee is charged for each reservation, payable on arrival.

Specific sites cannot be guaranteed; your site will be assigned upon your arrival. In some cases, reserved campsites may not be available until 4:00 p.m. on the day you arrive. Campsite reservations are held until 8:00 p.m. on arrival day. You must notify the park to hold your reservation beyond that time, or the campsite may be rented to someone else. If you cannot honor your reservation, please notify the park staff so that your campsite can be made available to others.

In most cases, reservations are taken only at the park for which the reservation is requested. There

A lifeguard makes a swimmin' hole safer, but it's always best to keep your guard up, too.

are exceptions to this: Jay Cooke accepts reservations for Moose Lake, and Tettegouche accepts reservations for Cascade River, George Crosby-Manitou, Judge Magney, and Temperance River state parks. Four state parks have special reservation phone numbers:

Bear Head Lake (218) 365-3150
Gooseberry Falls (218) 834-3787
Itasca (218) 266-3655
St. Croix (612) 384-6657

A brochure on the reservation system is available free from any state park or the DNR Information Center.

Permits and Fees

Daily or annual permits are required for all vehicles entering a state park. The one exception to this rule is on the first Sunday in June each year, which the DNR designates as Open House Day, with free admission to any of the state parks on that day. The annual permit, displayed on your windshield, gives you and everyone in your vehicle unlimited access to all 63 state parks for that year it was purchased. The annual permit costs $16, whereas a daily permit costs $3.25. Special permits are available for Minnesota senior citizens, handicapped citizens, second vehicles, and pre-arranged groups of 10 vehicles or more.

Camping fees are based on the type of facilities used. The fees differ for semi-modern sites, rustic

Glacial Lakes State Park (page 115) is one of more than 20 state parks that rent canoes. Minnesota is said to have 3,550 miles of canoeing waters. Perhaps you've noticed that folks in Minnesota who have a canoe on top of their car also have a smile on their face.

sites, electrical hook-ups, hike-in or canoe-in sites, and group campgrounds. Minnesota residents 65 or older or handicapped may camp for half-price the regular camping fees on Sunday through Thursday. A copy of the latest fee schedule for camping and entry permits is available from any state park or from the DNR Information Center. The annual vehicle permit may be purchased from any state park or by phone from the DNR Information Center. VISA or Mastercard is accepted.

State Park Rules

In order to protect the park and ensure its users a safe and enjoyable outdoor experience, rules are necessary. Although some parks have rules unique to their special situations, the following rules are basic to most parks:

▲ Camp only in designated locations.

▲ Noise at a level above that of a quiet conversation is prohibited between 10 p.m. and 8 a.m.

▲ The use of firearms, explosives, air guns, slingshots, traps, seines, nets, bows and arrows, and all other weapons is prohibited.

▲ Pets must be restrained on a leash no longer than six feet; they are not allowed in park buildings.

▲ Motor bikes and other licensed vehicles are allowed only on park roads, not trails. However, snowmobiles may use designated trails during winter.

▲ Do not pick or dig up plants, disturb or feed animals, or scavenge dead wood.

▲ Build fires only in fire rings or in fireplaces provided for that purpose. Portable stoves or grills are permitted.

▲ No intoxicating liquors may be consumed in the park.

▲ Camping permits expire at 4 p.m.

▲ Fishing conforming to Minnesota laws and rules is permitted in the waters adjacent to the state park.

▲ No person shall swim in a state park except at beaches designated for such use, and as directed by the lifeguard, if one is present.

▲ Daily or annual permits are required for all vehicles entering a state park.

State parks are administered by the DNR Division of Parks and Recreation. For general information on the state parks, write or call:

Minnesota Department of Natural Resources
Division of Parks and Recreation
Box 39, 500 Lafayette Road
St. Paul, MN 55155-4039
(612) 296-4776

Group Camps

Group camps, also called group centers, are available for groups of all kinds: family reunions, health and educational organizations, youth groups, college classes or a group of friends getting together. Centers can accommodate groups up to 215 people for a day, a weekend, or longer.

Three types of group camps are available for both day and overnight use: modern group centers, semi-modern group centers, and rustic camps. Modern group camps offer complete modern facilities from cabins and hot showers to dining halls and kitchens, plus private recreation areas. Six state parks have modern group centers: Lake Carlos (Region 1); St. Croix (Region 2); and Flandrau, Lake Shetek, Sibley, and Whitewater (Region 3). Whitewater's center is winterized for year-round use.

Semi-modern group camps offer you the same facilities as the modern camps, with the exception of lodging accommodations. Areas are available for tents or recreation vehicles. Three state parks have semi-modern group camps: Itasca and Lake Bemidji (Region 1), and Helmer Myre (Region 3).

Rustic group camps are available in most parks and offer an open area with tables, fire areas, toilets and a water source. All but nine state parks have rustic group camps. The parks that do not have rustic group camps are: Franz Jevne (Region 1); Banning, George H. Crosby-Manitou, Judge C. R. Magney, Moose Lake, Split Rock Lighthouse, Temperance River, and Tettegouche (Region 2); and Monson Lake (Region 3). The nine parks listed above with modern and semi-modern group centers also have rustic group camps available. For details on specific accommodations, fees, and availability, contact the park directly, or phone the DNR Information Center. A free brochure entitled *Group Centers* is also available.

The Passport Club

The Passport Club is a fun and easy way to keep a record of the different state parks you visit. The membership kit costs $4.95 and may be purchased at any park or from the DNR. As a club member, carry your passport with you on your state park visits. At each park, have your passport stamped by park staff as a record of your visit. After visiting 8, 16, 32 and 64* state parks, present your passport at any state park to receive free patches, nights of camping, posters and more. (*Note: An adjustment is being made for park number 64.) Get specific details by picking up a brochure on the Passport Club. What a neat incentive to keep exploring and visiting new state parks!

DNR Information Center

Reference has been made throughout this section on state parks to the DNR Information Center. The center can provide you with:
▲ Complete information and free state park maps and literature.
▲ Suggestions on what parks can meet your needs.
▲ Reports on snowmobile and cross-country ski trail conditions.
▲ Reports on river levels and conditions of state boating routes.
▲ Park permit and gift orders for credit card sales.
▲ Information on other DNR services, facilities, and regulations.
The center is open Monday through Friday, 8:00 a.m. to 4:30 p.m., and can be contacted at:
DNR Information Center
Box 40, 500 Lafayette Road
St. Paul, MN 55155-4040
Twin Cities: (612) 296-6157
MN toll free: 1-800-652-9747 (ask for DNR)

STATE FORESTS

Minnesota has many forests—the hardwood-covered hills in the southeast, the mix of pines and hardwoods in central Minnesota, and the boreal spruce and balsam fir of the north. Almost one-third of its total land area is covered with forests; it is the sixteenth most forested state in the nation. Much of this timberland lies within Minnesota's 56 state forests.

The Department of Natural Resources (DNR), Division of Forestry, manages over 3.2 million acres of land within state forest boundaries and more than 1.3 million acres of other state-owned land. The 56 state forests are managed by law to produce timber and other forest crops, protect watershed values, provide habitat for wildlife and plants, and provide outdoor recreation.

The DNR maintains over 50 recreation areas with campgrounds containing more than 800 campsites. Over 20 canoe campsites are located on lakes and canoe routes. These areas are primitive, designed to furnish only the basic needs for each activity. Campsites consist of a cleared area, fireplace, and table. In addition, vault toilets, level parking spurs, garbage containers, and drinking water are provided at campgrounds that charge a fee. Group

Gone for the day! These campers chose a beautiful campsite, but they chose to spend today exploring the backcountry. Their "home away from home" is waiting for them when they return.

camping areas have been developed at several campgrounds. Group camp fees are similar to those of the state parks. No fees are charged for other recreational use of state forests, but remember to pack out all your trash!

The state forests also provide about 250 picnic sites, more than 170 boat accesses and nearly 1,200 miles of hiking, snowmobiling, skiing and horse trails. Some forests have trails and camps specifically designed for horseback riders. Most state forest snowmobile trails are groomed. Many connect into state trails and local grants-in-aid trails, thus providing a system stretching thousands of miles. Trail maps can be obtained from the Area Forest Supervisor or from the DNR Information Center in St. Paul.

In addition, Minnesota's state forests contain over 2,000 miles of forest roads and thousands of logging trails that provide access to unlimited opportunities for recreationists to pursue a variety of unstructured outdoor activities such as berry picking, mushroom hunting, wildflower identification, and nature photography.

Registration is required on envelopes provided at each campground where a fee is charged. Sites are available on a first-come, first-served basis only. Group camp reservations are available by calling the office of the Area Forest Supervisor. Reservations are not taken except at group camps. Forest campground and day use areas are open officially from the first Saturday in May through the second Sunday in September, although the public is allowed access to these areas during the entire year. Any user of a state forest should remember that there are private lands within state forests. Respect landowner rights; always ask permission before entering private lands.

A partial list of rules governing the use of designated state forest campgrounds include the following:

- ▲ Camping is permitted only in designated camping areas.
- ▲ Camping is limited to a total period of 14 days in any one forest campground during the period when officially open, except with permission of the forest officer.
- ▲ Campers should pay the camping fee immediately upon occupying a campsite.
- ▲ The campsite must be occupied by a member of the party on the first night of the permit.
- ▲ Camping permits expire at 4:00 p.m.
- ▲ Only one individual, family, or group should occupy a single campsite. A group other than a family cannot exceed 8 people.
- ▲ Pets are permitted but should be effectively restrained by a portable enclosure or by a leash not exceeding six feet and should be personally attended.

The quiet hiker may have the good fortune of seeing "Bambi" along the trail. Look, but don't touch!

- ▲ Where firewood is provided at no charge, its use should be within reasonable limits.
- ▲ Boating and fishing conforming to Minnesota laws and rules are permitted in the waters adjacent to forest campgrounds and day-use areas.

The DNR Division of Forestry has a brochure entitled *Minnesota State Forest Campgrounds and Recreation Areas* that should be of interest to all outdoor enthusiasts. A map displays the location of each of the 56 state forests, as well as the sites of the campgrounds and day-use areas. The general location of the state forest snowmobile trails, hiking/ski trails, bicycle trails, and canoe routes are also indicated. A chart also displays the mileages of each of the trails and in which state forest each is located. The brochure may be obtained from any Area Forest Supervisor's office or from the DNR Information Center.

Detailed information on the 24 state forests that have campgrounds is found in this *Camper's Guide*. Region 1 includes 2 state forests; Region 2 has 12, and Region 3 includes 10 state forests that have developed campgrounds. Facilities, directions for traveling, a map, and the address and phone number of the Area Forest Supervisor is given for each state forest campground. This information should prove invaluable to you as you plan your next camping trip to a state forest.

For general Minnesota State Forest or general forestry information, write or call:

Minnesota Department of Natural Resources
Division of Forestry
Box 44, 500 Lafayette Rd.
St. Paul, MN 55155-4044
(612) 296-4491

NATIONAL FORESTS

Minnesota has two national forests within its boundaries—Chippewa National Forest and Superior National Forest. Together, they encompass a total of 4.6 million acres; however, some areas within the forest boundaries are privately owned. Eleven ranger districts administer 49 developed campgrounds that have a total of 1,270 individual campsites. In addition, over 3,000 lakes, countless miles of streams, 12 canoe routes (excluding those within the Boundary Waters Canoe Area), nearly 1,000 miles of multi-use trails, and some 600 dispersed primitive campsites are available for recreational use.

Detailed information for each of the 49 developed campgrounds is given by ranger districts; Chippewa National Forest is in Region 1 and Superior National Forest is in Region 2. Other information that is basic to both national forests is given here rather than repeated for each forest.

The main camping season is from mid-May through September. Although most campgrounds remain open for public use after the regular season,

The Wilderness Drive at Itasca State Park (page 44) has numerous points of interest along the way. Among them is Minnesota's record red (Norway) pine. Scars on the trunk indicate that this 300-year-old tree has survived six forest fires.

water pumps are shut down and garbage collection is discontinued. Campsites are available on a first-come, first-served basis. Some campgrounds are operated by concessionaire and will take reservations for campsites as well as first-come, first-served. All campgrounds limit campers to a 14-day stay. When this 2-week limit is reached, the camper is required to move to another campground unless special permission has been secured.

Campground facilities vary from flush toilets and showers to rustic campgrounds with vault toilets and handpump. Each campsite has a picnic table, fireplace, and tent pad. Most units have a parking spur to accommodate trailers up to 22 feet long. Some units are designed as carry-in tent sites. Sewage and electrical hook-ups are not provided. Most camp units are limited to one family only. Many of the campgrounds have facilities to accommodate the disabled.

A camping fee is charged in the developed campgrounds. Golden Age and Golden Access Passports are honored and Forest Camp Stamps may be used. For those who want to "get away from it all," hundreds of dispersed campsites exist. These sites are free of charge and have limited or no facilities. Camping is prohibited in day-use areas such as parking lots, boat landings, and picnic grounds.

There are no lifeguards on duty at forest campgrounds. Pets must be on a leash. Firearms cannot be used in developed recreation areas. Minnesota licenses are required if you plan to hunt or fish in the forest. Canoes and boats must be registered. Maps of each forest are available for $2.00 from the national forest offices and ranger stations. The maps show roads not on most road maps, so they are invaluable and necessary for visitors wishing to explore the backcountry.

Visitors to a national forest are encouraged to visit either the office of the forest supervisor or the individual ranger district offices. They are able to supply you with numerous brochures on the various recreational activities, as well as give information on such items as road conditions, weather, campgrounds, dispersed camping areas, and trails. For your convenience, addresses and phone numbers are included for each national forest.

National Forest Camp Stamps

The U.S. Forest Service has a program called "Camp Stamps" that can save you 15% of the fee charged for use of national forest campgrounds.

Here's how it works: Anytime *before* you visit the national forest campground, purchase camp stamps at any forest service office or at selected retail outlets. You will only pay 85% of the stamps' face value. Upon arriving at the national forest campground, select your campsite, return to the self-service fee station, and follow the posted instructions for using your camp stamps to pay your fee. Not only do camp stamps save you money, they are also convenient in that there is no need for you to have the correct change for your campground fee. They do not expire and are good until used.

Camp stamps can be used along with Golden Age and Golden Access Passports. When paying the campsite fee, a passport holder must place only half the otherwise required number of camp stamps on the back of the fee envelope. The passport user must have in possession a valid passport at all times.

There are several things to remember about camp stamps:

▲ Camp stamps can be used only at national forest campgrounds.

▲ The prior purchase of camp stamps does not guarantee the availability of a campsite. Most national forest campgrounds are still first-come, first-served.

▲ If you don't buy camp stamps before you visit a national forest campground, you may still pay your camping fee with cash or check at the entrance fee station, but you will have to pay the full fee. The only way to get the 15% discount is through the advance purchase of camp stamps.

Camp stamps may be purchased at selected retail outlets, all regional and national forest headquarters, at most ranger district headquarters, and other local forest service offices.

U.S. ARMY CORPS OF ENGINEERS' LAKES ———————

The Mississippi River Headwaters area encompasses hundreds of lakes, streams, and rivers scattered among timbered, rolling hills in a sizable section of north central Minnesota. The area is recognized nationwide for its natural beauty, abundant fish and wildlife, and unsurpassed, four-season activities: swimming, boating, camping, picnicking, hiking, snowmobiling, hunting, cross-country skiing, and ice fishing.

Within this area are six major lakes: Winnibigoshish and Pokegama on the Mississippi River's main stem, and Leech, Big Sandy, Gull, and Whitefish Chain of Lakes (Pine River) on its tributaries. These lakes, impounded by Corps dams, provide flood control, produce a natural environment for fish and wildlife, and provide outstanding opportunities for water based recreation activities.

A recreation area with a developed campground is located at each of these six lakes in the Mississippi Headwaters area. Fees are charged for camping. No reservations are accepted, with the exception of a handicap accessible camp site available at each recreation area. It may be reserved in advance by contacting the Resource Manager's Office. Camping is permitted only at designated sites. There is a 14-day camping limit during any 30-day period; Golden Age and Golden Access Passports are honored.

Pets are not allowed on swimming beaches and should be penned, caged, physically restrained, or

Mississippi River Headwaters Area

1—Leech Lake Recreation Area
2—Lake Winnibigoshish Recreation Area
3—Pokegama Lake Recreation Area
4—Sandy Lake Recreation Area
5—Ronald Louis Cloutier Recreation Area
6—Terry R. Johnson Recreation Area

on a leash less than six feet long in any developed recreation area. Refer to the facility list for each recreation area for information regarding the number of camping sites, availability of electricity, showers, trailer dump station, swim beach, boat ramp, etc. For additional information, contact either the Resource Manager's Office at the specific recreation area or:

St. Paul District
U.S. Army Corps of Engineers
1135 U.S. Post Office & Custom House
St. Paul, MN 55101
(612) 725-7506

FEDERAL RECREATION PASSPORT PROGRAM

Some federal parks, refuges, and facilities can be entered and used free of charge. Other areas and facilities require payment of entrance fees, user fees, special recreation permit fees, or some combination. A 1987 brochure by the U.S. Department of the Interior entitled *Federal Recreation Passport Program* explains the five programs. Briefly stated, the three passports most beneficial to park visitors in Minnesota are as follows:

Golden Eagle Passport

An annual entrance pass to those national parks, monuments, historic sites, recreation areas, and national wildlife refuges that charge entrance fees. It admits the permit holder and accompanying persons in a private, noncommercial vehicle. For those not traveling by private car, it admits the permit holder and family group. Cost, $25; good for one calendar year (January 1 through December 31); permits unlimited entries to all federal entrance fee areas.

Golden Age Passport

A free lifetime entrance pass for citizens or permanent residents of the United States who are 62 years or older. Also provides 50% discount on federal use fees charged for facilities and services except those provided by private concessionaires. Must be obtained in person, with proof of age.

Golden Access Passport

A free lifetime entrance pass for citizens or permanent residents of the U.S. who have been medically determined to be blind or permanently disabled and, as a result, are eligible to receive benefits under federal law. Offers same benefits as Golden Age Passport. Must be obtained in person, with proof of eligibility.

Locations where these three passes are obtainable include all National Park System areas where entrance fees are charged, all National Forest Service supervisor's offices, and most Forest Service ranger station offices.

MINNESOTA TRAILS

Minnesotans are fortunate, indeed, to have a State Trail system, and access to several thousand miles of trails: self-guiding, hiking, backpacking, bicycle, horseback riding, cross-country ski, snowmobile, and canoe. Information pertinent to each type of trail is given in the following pages. There are two major sources of information (maps, booklets, brochures, etc.) for all these trails:

Minnesota Office of Tourism
375 Jackson St., 250 Skyway Level
St. Paul, MN 55101
Twin Cities: (612) 296-5029
In Minnesota: 1-800-652-9747
Outside Minnesota: 1-800-328-1461

Horses need a lunch break too! There are over 250 miles of horseback riding trails in the state parks; 14 of the parks have designated areas for horse camping.

DNR Information Center
500 Lafayette Road, Box 40
St. Paul, MN 55155-4040
Twin cities: (612) 296-6157
In Minnesota (ask for DNR): 1-800-652-9747

SELF-GUIDING TRAILS

Twenty-seven state parks in Minnesota have self-guiding trails totaling 39.5 miles. Self-guiding trails are of two main types: those that use interpretive signs along the trail and those that provide trail-guide booklets to be read along the way. When interpretive signs are used, they are placed at points of interest on the trail. On other trails, booklets containing numbered paragraphs that correspond to numbered posts along the trail are used.

With either method, self-guiding trails are popular because they allow park visitors to set their own pace for learning and hiking. The trails can be especially enjoyable for parents and children. They are also a cost-effective means for a park staff to provide interpretive information to a large number of visitors.

Each self-guiding trail offers an experience unique to the park where the trail is located. The information may identify flowers or trees, speak of wildlife habitat, glacial geology, wetland ecology, or prairie management; or reveal a historical event that occurred in that area.

State parks that have self-guiding trails are listed below by regions. For the length of each trail and other details, refer to the specific listing within a particular region.

Region 1

Buffalo River	Lake Carlos
Hayes Lake	Maplewood
Itasca	Mille Lacs Kathio
Lake Bemidji	Old Mill
Lake Bronson	Schoolcraft

Region 2

Banning	Scenic
Gooseberry Falls	Tettegouche
St. Croix	

Region 3

Afton	O. L. Kipp
Camden	Sibley
Flandrau	Upper Sioux Agency
Glacial Lakes	Whitewater
Helmer Myre	Wild River
Lake Louise	William O'Brien

Two other approaches to self-guided activities are used at Itasca State Park (Region 1) and Interstate

World-famous glacial potholes can be viewed along this self-guiding trail at Interstate State Park (page 117). The deepest one that has been measured accurately, the "Bottomless Pit," is more than 60 feet deep and 12–15 feet wide.

State Park (Region 3). Itasca has a 10-mile Wilderness Drive appropriately signed to be used with an auto-tour guide booklet. Visitors who use this guide booklet are able to learn about the majestic pines, archaeological sites, and forest ecology as they travel in the comfort of their own vehicle. At Interstate, visitors walking along the Pothole Trail may take along a cassette player and tape explaining the geological history of the St. Croix River.

STATE TRAILS

In 1973, the Division of Parks and Recreation of the Minnesota Department of Natural Resources (DNR), was legislatively authorized to coordinate a statewide recreational trail system. An extensive system of state trails, designed for all types of users, is being developed which will serve as the nucleus of a statewide network of trails. To date, 12 multiple-use state trails have been authorized.

When fully developed, these trails will provide nearly 1,000 miles for bicycling, hiking, ski touring, snow shoeing, horseback riding, and snowmobiling. Portions of trail right-of-ways of some trails are not presently owned by the state; several of the trails are incomplete. Seven of the trails follow abandoned railroad grades. In some instances, separate trail treadways are being developed to avoid conflicting recreation uses: one treadway is surfaced with a bituminous pavement for bicyclists, hikers, and snowmobilers; the other for horseback riders and skiers. Trail bikes and other all-terrain vehicles

(ATV's) are not permitted on state trails. Overnight camping and campfires are permitted only at designated campsites. Trail shelters are located along most of the trails.

Another type of trail is provided through the Minnesota Trail Assistance Program. This program gives grants in aid to trail user groups and local governments to acquire, develop, and maintain trails for snowmobiling and cross-country skiing. Grants-in-aid trails have been established throughout Minnesota and connect to many state trails, state park trails, state forest trails, and national forest trails.

Since trail users may choose to base-camp at one of the state parks, state forests, or national forest campgrounds, this *Camper's Guide* presents the general location of the state trails by regions. Pocket-sized maps showing state trail routes and permitted uses are available free from the DNR Information Center. Information on the Fire State Trail and the Carlton-West Duluth State Trail are included in the trail brochure for the Minnesota-Wisconsin State Trail. Although all trails are multi-use trails, some appear to be used by a particular group(s) of users more than others. These distinct uses are discussed in the sections that follow. Approximate mileages of completed sections of each of

the 12 state trails, according to DNR materials, is also given.

Region 1
Heartland (51 miles)
Region 2
Arrowhead (120 miles)
Carlton-West Duluth (14.5 miles)
Fire (36 miles)
Minnesota-Wisconsin Border (74 miles)
North Shore (154 miles)
Taconite (168 miles)
Region 3
Douglas (13 miles)
Luce Line (55 miles)
Minnesota Valley (34 miles)
Root River (30 miles)
Sakatah Singing Hills (39 miles)

The DNR Trails and Waterways Unit was organized in 1979 to meet the growing public demand for trail and water recreation opportunities. The unit provides services and information to Minnesota's canoeists, boaters, snowmobilers, skiers, hikers, bicyclists and horseback riders. For general information on trails and waterways, write or call:

Minnesota Department of Natural Resources
Trails and Waterways Unit
Box 52, 500 Lafayette Road
St. Paul, MN 55155-4052
(612) 296-6699

HIKING AND BACKPACKING TRAILS

Hundreds of miles of foot trails are located in state parks, state forests, the two national forests, the two national parks, and other state and nationally administered areas in Minnesota. These trails range from easy, well maintained trails suitable for short day-hikes to rugged trails offering longer trips for experienced hikers and backpackers. One-half of the 16-page booklet produced by the Minnesota Office of Tourism entitled *Explore Minnesota Canoeing, Hiking, and Backpacking*, addresses trails suitable for day-hikes or backpacking trips. The booklet covers a sampler of 50 trails throughout the state. Anyone interested in exploring the scenic areas and backcountry of Minnesota by foot should definitely obtain a copy of this booklet, available either from the Office of Tourism or from the DNR.

For an overview of the many trails available for hiking and backpacking, consider the following facts:

Minnesota Recreational Trail System

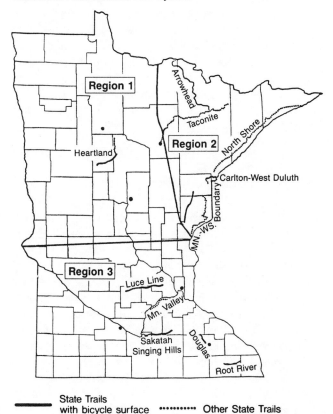

—————— State Trails
with bicycle surface   ·············· Other State Trails

▲ Every single one of the 63 state parks has a foot trail according to the DNR's *Guide to Minnesota State Parks*. In distance, they range from the 1-mile trails found at Franz Jevne State Park and Monson Lake State Park to the 127 miles of trails available at St. Croix State Park. The trails total almost 900 miles.

▲ Designated hiking trails are available on more than 15 state forests and total more than 300 miles. In addition, miles of forest roads and thousands of logging trails exist.

▲ In the Superior National Forests' "Recreation Trail Index," 33 designated trails are listed totaling almost 450 miles. The Boundary Waters Canoe Area Wilderness (BWCA) lies within a portion of the Superior National Forest; permits are required for overnight use between May 1 and September 30. Several popular wilderness hiking trails that lie within the BWCA include the 38-mile Border Route Trail, the 14-mile Angleworm Trail, and the 16-mile Snowbank-Old Pine Hiking Trail.

▲ The Chippewa National Forest has 25 designated trails with mileages totaling over 250. Trails that are suitable for extended wilderness backpack trips include the 68-mile North Country Trail, which will someday run from the Appalachian Trail in New York to the Lewis and Clark Trail in North Dakota; the 22-mile Cut Foot Sioux Trail, which follows the Continental Divide; and the 18-mile Suomi Hills Trail.

▲ The two national parks in Minnesota offer some interesting trail options. The Grand Portage National Monument has an 8-mile trail that follows the route of historic portages of fur traders. The Voyageurs National Park has 32 miles of developed and maintained trails where the trailheads are accessible by water only.

▲ The northern section of the 150-mile long North Shore State Trail is most suitable for hiking and backpacking. This 70-mile section has been one of Minnesota's longest backpacking opportunities.

▲ A new trail, The Superior Hiking Trail, will outdistance all other Minnesota trails, once it is completed. The trail traverses the ridgeline roughly paralleling Lake Superior, within one or two miles of the lake. Several sections of the trail are presently completed. Hikers and backpackers will want to stay abreast of information on this trail, and perhaps, offer support by joining the Superior Hiking Trail Association. The association needs volunteers; active involvement of its members is needed to accomplish their goals. When completed, the trail will connect seven state parks, a national forest, two state forests, and other lands, through 250 miles of rough and exciting terrain. The trail will potentially connect with the Voyageur Trail from Thunder Bay to Sault Ste. Marie, and the North Country Trail from New York to North Dakota, which passes the south shore of Lake Superior. For information, write:

> Superior Hiking Trail Asscoiation
> Box 2157
> Tofte, MN 55615

Most backpackers are probably aware that many backcountry campsites exist on national forest lands. However, they may not know about the many opportunities in the state parks for camping away from the activity of a busy campground. Many state parks have walk-in campsites that are less than ¼ mile from the parking area. These sites are more rustic. Split Rock Lighthouse State Park, a walk-in campground, has a unique arrangement where campers park their vehicles in the parking lot, then load their gear into lightweight carts, and wheel their gear down gravel trails to pre-selected campsites. State parks with *walk-in sites* are:

Hikers enjoy a scenic tree-lined trail in Sakatah Lake State Park (page 131). This park serves as a convenient base camp for those wishing to travel the 42-mile multiple-use Sakatah Singing Hills State Trail (pages 12–13).

Region 1
  Hayes Lake (2)
  Maplewood (3)
Region 2
  Gooseberry Falls (3)
  St. Croix (4)
  Split Rock Lighthouse (20)
Region 3
  Beaver Creek (6)
  Frontenac (6)
  Kilen Woods (4)
  Lake Shetak (10)
  Minnesota Valley (12)
  Whitewater (6)
  Wild River (1)

Backpack sites are designed for those seeking a wilderness experience. At state parks, these secluded sites are at least ¼ mile and as many as 10 miles from the parking area. They, too, are more rustic; drinking water may have to be carried in by campers. State parks with *backpack sites* are:

Region 1
  Itasca (4)
Region 2
  Bear Head Lake (5)
  Cascade River (5)
  *George H. Crosby-Manitou (21)
  Jay Cooke (4)
  St. Croix (2)
  Savanna Portage (4)
  Scenic (7)
  Split Rock Lighthouse (4)
Region 3
  *Afton (24)
  Fort Ridgely (4)
  Glacial Lakes (2)
  Helmer Myre (4)
  *Lake Maria (11)
  Wild River (4)

The three parks noted with the asterisk (*) are considered backpack only campgrounds; they do not have drive-in campsites. Split Rock Lighthouse should be added to this list since only walk-in sites and backpack sites are available.

Note that the first batch of 12 state parks list 77 walk-in campsites, while the second listing of 15 state parks offers 105 campsites for the backpacker. These types of sites are obviously in the minority, since there are over 3,800 drive-in campsites available, but it's good to know that parks are providing this type of camping opportunity for those who prefer the wilderness experience.

Three types of trails are available to bicyclists: surfaced bicycle trails; the internal roads that may be suitable for cycling during the less busy season; and the off-road bicycle (ORB) trails.

BICYCLE TRAILS

According to the *Explore Minnesota Biking* brochure published by the Minnesota Office of Tourism, Minnesota is biking country! The bicycle touring season generally begins in late April and lasts through mid-October. There are, indeed, many biking opportunities in the state. Among them are the surfaced bicycle trails, off-road bicycle trails, and low-traffic internal roads in some 20 state parks; and seven state trails that have been developed for bicycling on abandoned railroad right-of-ways.

The facilities chart of the brochure entitled *Guide to Minnesota State Parks* includes the number of miles of bike trails. This information usually refers to the miles of surfaced bicycle trails. A park's internal roads may also be suitable for bicycling during the less busy season.

In addition to these trails and to accommodate the growing demand for off-road bicycle trails (ORB), 14 state parks designated some trails for ORB use beginning in the fall of 1986. During the trial use period, designated trails are to be checked to determine the impact of bicycle use, and visitors will be surveyed to identify potential user conflicts. As a result, additional ORB trails may be opened while some may be discontinued. The designated ORB trails are not paved and are not easy to ride with standard narrow tires; mountain bikes are needed. The trail surface is mowed grass or compacted soil. Off-road cyclists should remember that bicycles in the backcountry are a new experience for horses and hikers and, therefore, should be sensitive to their presence.

The surfaces of the seven state trails are either blacktop or crushed limestone. The Office of Tour-

Minnesota Bicycle Trails

		Miles of Surfaced Bicycle Trails	Miles of Off-Road Bicycle Trails	Miles of Low-Traffic Internal Road Connections
Region 3	Hayes Lake State Park	1	4	3
	HEARTLAND STATE TRAIL	27		
	Itasca State Park	6½		10½
	Lake Bemidji State Park	1	5	
	Lake Bronson State Park	5	4	
	Maplewood State Park		10½	13½
Region 2	CARLTON-WEST DULUTH STATE TRAIL	14½		
	FIRE STATE TRAIL	32		
	Goosberry Falls State Park		10	
	Jay Cooke State Park	*	5½	
	McCarthy Beach State Park		12	
	St. Croix State Park	6½	23½	
	Savanna Portage State Park		10	4
	Scenic State Park		5	
	Split Rock Lighthouse State Park		6	
Region 1	Afton State Park	4		
	Camden State Park		3½	4
	DOUGLAS STATE TRAIL	13		
	Ft. Snelling State Park	5		
	Helmer Myre State Park		7	3
	LUCE LINE STATE TRAIL	37		
	Minnesota Valley State Park & STATE TRAIL	4	25	
	ROOT RIVER STATE TRAIL	30		
	Sakatah Lake State Park	*4		
	SAKATAH SINGING HILLS STATE TRAIL	39		
	Sibley State Park	5		
	William O'Brien State Park	2		

*Access to STATE BICYCLE TRAILS

Bicycles can be rented at Itasca State Park (page 44) by the hour or by the day . . . or you can bring your own. What better way to see the sights!

ism's biking brochure has a brief description of each of these seven state trails. Small, pocket-sized trail maps are also available free from the DNR Information Center. The Minnesota Bicycle Trails chart has been compiled from various sources from the DNR and Office of Tourism to display the mileages of these 27 bicycle trails.

Other bicycling opportunities in the state include roads and trails in state forests; trails that have been partially funded with state money, such as the 19-mile Cannon Valley Trail between Red Wing and Cannon, southeast of the Twin Cities; and other routes that follow country roads.

Bicycles and most other types of motorized and non-motorized use are permitted on state forest trails unless posted otherwise. State forests do not have trails or roads specifically designated for ORB use. Bicyclists should note the other types of use on roads and trails and the terrain they traverse before using trails. This will help avoid conflicts with other recreational trail users and damage to the trail itself. Maps for many of the state forest snowmobile and ski trails, some of which may be suitable for ORB, are available from the DNR Information Center. Bicyclists should contact the appropriate Area Forest Supervisor for detailed information on the specific road or trail in question.

Bike routes along country roads can be planned with the help of *Explore Minnesota Bikeways* maps. The Minnesota Department of Transportation has developed a series of maps covering the entire state that rate roads for cycling. An initial series of 54 maps exist, as well as 2 new maps, one covering the southeast quadrant of Minnesota and another covering the northeast quarter of the state. East Metro and West Metro maps are also available on the Twin Cities area. These maps may be purchased, for a very nominal fee, from bike shops or directly from:

Minnesota Department of Transportation
John Ireland Boulevard
Room B-20
St. Paul, MN 55155
(612) 296-2216

The Office of Tourism's biking brochure outlines four suggested trips that explore very different areas of Minnesota: the North Shore of Lake Superior, the northern pine and lakes area of north central Minnesota, the Pipestone countryside of the southwest, and the bluff country of the southeast. Each of these routes follows country roads. This free 8-page brochure also includes a map and brochure order form of the free bicycling materials from the DNR as well as the Bikeways map order form from the Minnesota Department of Transportation. Other information includes some safety hints, bike rental places, and names and addresses of where you can obtain additional information on biking in Minnesota.

HORSEBACK RIDING TRAILS ——————

Eighteen state parks have designated trails for horseback riding ranging in length from the 3-mile trail at Hayes Lake State Park to the 75 miles of trails at St. Croix State Park. Fourteen of the state parks have designated areas for horse camping. Since accommodations may vary, contact the individual park for specifics. The state parks having horseback riding trails totaling 259 miles, are listed below by regions. All of the parks have horse camping facilities except those marked with an asterisk (*).

Region 1

Hayes Lake	Mille Lacs Kathio
Lake Carlos	*Zippel Bay
Maplewood	

Region 2

*Jay Cooke
St. Croix

Region 3

*Afton	*Lake Maria
Forestville	Minnesota Valley
Fort Ridgely	Sibley
Glacial Lakes	Upper Sioux Agency
Lac Qui Parle	Wild River
Lake Louise	

According to the DNR State Trail maps and other DNR materials on horseback riding, portions of seven of the state trails have been developed with the horseback rider in mind: in Region 1, the Heartland State Trail (44 miles); in Region 2, the Minnesota-Wisconsin Boundary State Trail (51 miles), North Shore State Trail (92 miles), and Taconite State Trail (32 miles); and in Region 3, the Douglas State Trail (12 miles), Luce Line State Trail (15 miles), and Minnesota Valley State Trail (30 miles).

More than ten state forests have designated trails for horseback riding, while in several other state forests, the trails and roads can be used by horses but are not signed for that purpose. Vehicles are permitted on these roads so horseback riders should be alert for their presence. The State Forest Supervisor should be contacted for complete information on the horseback riding trails and accommodations for horseback camping. Policies change from time to time; it would pay to obtain the latest information prior to travel. The following state forests allow horseback riding, and those with an asterisk (*) have accommodations for horseback camping:

Region 1

*Beltrami Island
*Buena Vista
*Paul Bunyan
*Huntersville
  Land O'Lakes
*Pillsbury
  White Earth

Region 2

*General C. C. Andrews
  George Washington
  Kabetogama
*St. Croix

Region 3

Richard J. Doer Memorial Hardwood (trails on 7 units; horse camping on 3 units)
Sand Dunes

CROSS-COUNTRY SKI TRAILS ——————

According to the 50-page guide to cross-country ski trails, entitled *Explore Minnesota on Skis*, Min-

These skiers may be a little chilly now, but they'll warm up fast once they hit the trail.

nesota has over 1,800 miles of trails. This guide book, produced by the Minnesota Office of Tourism, and available from them or the DNR Information Center, lists 275 different ski trails/areas. There are cross-country ski trails in virtually every part of Minnesota. All but six of the 63 state parks have ski trails totaling over 540 miles, and 12 state forests have 160 miles of trails.

Five of the 12 state trails have large portions designated for cross-country skiing: the Heartland State Trail (28 miles) in Region 1; and the Douglas State Trail (13 miles), Luce Line State Trail (6.5 miles), Minnesota Valley State Trail (17.5 miles), and Root River State Trail (30 miles) in Region 3. The Chippewa National Forest has eight major ski trails that total 150 miles. Among them are the 22-mile Cut Foot Sioux National Recreation Trail that follows the Continental Divide and the 68-mile North Country National Scenic Trail, a national trail eventually to connect New York and North Dakota.

According to the Minnesota office of Tourism's guide, the Superior National Forest has 15 cross-country ski trails that total nearly 170 miles. However, according to the *Recreation Trail Index* for the Superior National Forest, there are actually more than 450 miles of skiing available on 33 different trails, including more than 200 miles of trails that are generally groomed. This northeast area of the state has the longest networks of trails. Among them are the Border Route Trail (38 miles), Upper Gunflint Lake Trail (62 miles), Grand Portage Ski Trail (44 miles), and the North Shore Mountains Trail (75 miles).

Minnesota's cross country ski season varies within the state. The southeast averages a minimum of six inches snow cover for 43 days; the northeast, around the Gunflint Trail has an average of 160 days of six inches, and 150 days of at least twelve inches of snow.

Snow depth information is available from the Minnesota Travel Information Center, 24 hours a day, during snow season:

> (612) 296-5029—in the Twin Cities
> 1-800-652-9747—toll-free in Minnesota
> 1-800-328-1461—toll-free nationally

Statewide road condition information is available from the Minnesota Department of Transportation: (612) 296-3076.

The State of Minnesota requires a cross-country ski pass for skiers aged 16-64 who use any non-federal public trail designated and promoted for cross-country skiing. Each trail listed in the guide book notes whether a ski pass is required. The cost of an annual license is $5.30 for an individual, and $7.95 for a husband and wife. A three-year pass is $14.84 for individuals, or $22.26 for husband and wife. Licenses are valid July 1–June 30 of the following year. Skiers may purchase a daily permit for $1.06. Tax is included in all of the above prices. The funds are used exclusively to maintain existing trails and to develop additional trail miles. Ski passes are available from:

> DNR Bureau of Licenses
> Box 26, 500 Lafayette Road
> St. Paul, MN 55155-4026

Or, phone 1-800-652-9747 (in Minnesota) or 1-800-328-1461 (outside Minnesota) and ask for "Ski Pass." You can even pay for "Ski Pass" with VISA or Mastercard. The licenses can also be purchased at any state park, county auditor, or other participating public and private vendor such as trail operators or sporting goods stores.

The trail guide gives the length of the trail in kilometers, notes whether the trail is groomed, signed, degree of difficulty, whether an additional fee is charged (such as a state park entrance fee), and whether a map/brochure is available. The availability of toilets and parking within a quarter-mile of the trailhead is also noted, as well as the location, trail connections, services, and features of the trail. If you plan to enjoy the Minnesota outdoors this winter via ski-touring, you definitely need a copy of *Explore Minnesota on Skis* in order to determine all of your options!

SNOWMOBILE TRAILS

There are 11,600 miles of marked and groomed snowmobile trails in Minnesota to accommodate a wide range of experiences. The terrain is as diverse as snowmobilers themselves. The 50-page *Explore Minnesota by Snowmobile* booklet, produced by the Minnesota Office of Tourism, describes 260 trail systems in Minnesota. It provides descriptions of trails in northern Minnesota, southern Minnesota, and the Twin Cities metropolitian area. The guide gives the length of the trail in miles, notes whether the trail is groomed, signed, and whether a map/brochure is available. The availability of toilets, parking, food, and gasoline facilities within a quarter-mile of the trailhead is also noted, as well as the location, trail connections, services, and features of the trail.

Forty of the 63 state parks have snowmobile trails totaling 475 miles, and more than 25 state forests have trails totaling over 1,000 miles. Eleven of the 12 state trails account for more than 750 miles of snowmobile trails; Root River is the only state trail not designated for snowmobiling. Over 160 miles of trails are available in the Chippewa National Forest, and, according to the *Recreation Trail Index* for the Superior National Forest, there are 175 miles of snowmobiling available on 11 different trails.

The vast majority of Minnesota's snowmobile trails cross private land by permission granted to local units of governments and through the management of snowmobile clubs. Riders using snowmobile trails should respect the rights of the many hundreds of private landowners who have made this system possible.

Snowmobiles must be registered by the Minnesota Department of Natural Resources (DNR). One of the only exemptions to this registration is for snowmobiles registered in other states, but in Minnesota for fewer than 30 consecutive days. The monies generated by snowmobile registrations are combined with a portion of the state gasoline tax in a special dedicated account. The bulk of this money is used to assist the development and maintenance of about 9,000 miles of DNR grants-in-aid trails. The snowmobile registration costs $18.00 for three years, and is available from the Commissioner of Natural Resources through the

DNR Bureau of Licenses
Box 26, 500 Lafayette Road
St. Paul, MN 55155-4026

or, from the Commissioner of Public Safety through any authorized deputy registrar of motor vehicles. A state park annual or daily permit is required if you trailer your snowmobile into a state park.

Snow depth information is available as described earlier under "Cross-Country Ski Trails." The *Explore Minnesota by Snowmobile* booklet is available from the Minnesota Office of Tourism or the DNR Information Center. This guide, along with maps available from the DNR and other sources, should prove quite helpful in planning your snowmobile trips each snow season.

CANOEING IN MINNESOTA

CANOE ROUTES

Whether it's spring, summer, or fall, canoeing is a great way to explore Minnesota—the land of sky-tinted waters and 10,000 lakes. Each season of the year has its own mystique when you're observing its moods from a canoe. Nineteen rivers have been designated as canoe and boating routes by the state, and are managed by the Minnesota Department of Natural Resources. Canoe camping is possible on most of the rivers. Designated campsites have a fire ring, pit toilet, and table. Most do not provide pumped water. Wilderness rivers do not have as many designated campsites; consequently, good backcountry camping skills are required.

In addition to the 19 rivers managed by the DNR, there are 4 canoe routes managed by the Forest Service. Vermillion River is on the Superior National Forest and Inguadona River, Rice River and Turtle River are on the Chippewa National Forest. Rice River is not regularly maintained; canoeists should watch for down trees.

Detailed, pocket-sized maps of the 19 state canoe routes and the Vermillion River are available free from the DNR. These maps provide mile by mile information including accesses, campsites, towns, road crossings, rapids, portages and other information. Maps of the other three rivers are available from the Chippewa National Forest.

Interstate State Park (page 117), located along the St. Croix National Scenic Riverway, has a canoe rental as well as a shuttle service available. Shouldn't they be wearing those lifejackets?

A 16-page brochure entitled *Canoeing, Hiking, and Backpacking in Minnesota* is available from the Minnesota Office of Tourism. Eight pages of this very informative brochure are devoted to canoeing. River descriptions of the 23 rivers (see map) are given, as well as safety tips, rapids classification system, and a very extensive list of canoe rentals and outfitters located near the various rivers. So that you may know the general characteristics

Minnesota Canoe Routes

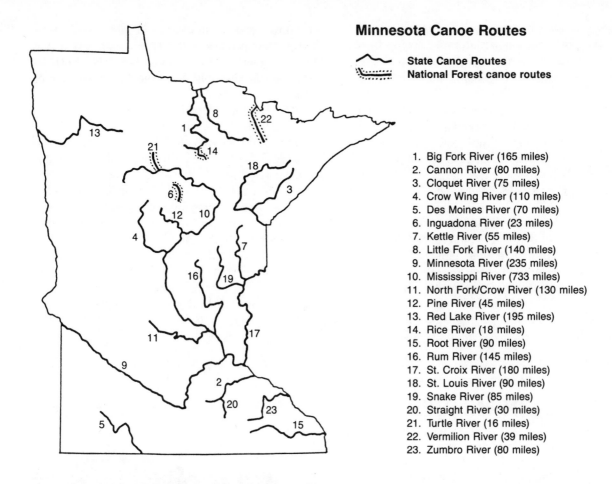

⌒ **State Canoe Routes**
╲╌╌╌ **National Forest canoe routes**

1. Big Fork River (165 miles)
2. Cannon River (80 miles)
3. Cloquet River (75 miles)
4. Crow Wing River (110 miles)
5. Des Moines River (70 miles)
6. Inguadona River (23 miles)
7. Kettle River (55 miles)
8. Little Fork River (140 miles)
9. Minnesota River (235 miles)
10. Mississippi River (733 miles)
11. North Fork/Crow River (130 miles)
12. Pine River (45 miles)
13. Red Lake River (195 miles)
14. Rice River (18 miles)
15. Root River (90 miles)
16. Rum River (145 miles)
17. St. Croix River (180 miles)
18. St. Louis River (90 miles)
19. Snake River (85 miles)
20. Straight River (30 miles)
21. Turtle River (16 miles)
22. Vermilion River (39 miles)
23. Zumbro River (80 miles)

of these 23 rivers, and the opportunities that exist for outdoor recreation, a thumbnail sketch is given. The following information has been taken from the brochure.

Many Minnesota rivers offer easygoing canoeing, with long stretches of water with no rapids and occasional small rapids. In the north, the Crow Wing, upper Mississippi, Inguadona, Pine, Rice, lower Rum, St. Croix and Turtle rivers all have long stretches suitable for novice paddlers under normal flow conditions.

In the southeast, the Cannon, Root, Straight, and Zumbro rivers all offer easygoing canoeing. The Minnesota and Des Moines rivers in the southwest are good for novices, and in the Twin Cities area, the North Fork Crow is a good choice. All of these rivers are good for day trips. There are designated campsites on all of these rivers except the Straight.

Several Minnesota rivers have stretches that offer a bit more challenge for the canoeist of intermediate skill. These canoeists may enjoy stretches of the Big Fork, Cloquet, Kettle, Mississippi, Pine, Red Lake, Rum, St. Croix, St. Louis, Snake and Vermillion rivers. There are designated campsites available on all of these rivers.

Expert canoeists are those who have had extensive experience and instruction in canoeing under a variety of conditions and can negotiate difficult rapids and large bodies of water. Expert canoeists may be challenged by rapids on the Kettle, Little Fork, Snake, and Vermillion rivers, as well as other rivers during early spring high water levels. There are designated campsites on all of these rivers except the Little Fork.

The Big Fork, Cloquet, St. Louis, and Vermillion rivers are all good for extended wilderness canoe trips. Camping canoeists on the Big Fork, Cloquet, and Little Fork should have good backcountry skills because of the nature of the available campsites.

Weekly water level reports are prepared for designated canoe rivers from May to October by the DNR. The reports note whether the water levels are sufficient for canoeing or whether they are dangerously deep and swift. Call: 296-6157 in the Twin Cities area or 1-800-652-9747, toll free from Minnesota. Ask for the DNR Information Center.

All canoes used on Minnesota waters must be licensed, whether they are owned by a Minnesota resident or a resident of another state. The canoe license costs $7.00 and is valid for three years; validation decals must be placed on the canoe. Those visiting from other states with a canoe license from their own state do not need to purchase a Minnesota canoe license; their own state's canoe license is valid for 90 days in Minnesota.

There are many other canoeing opportunities in Minnesota in addition to these canoe routes. A U.S. Army Corps of Engineers' brochure describes a 14½-mile route on the Gull River from Gull Lake Dam to the Fisherman's Bridge on CR 36 south of SH 210. A few state parks have a short canoe route on lakes and streams in their immediate area. The Superior National Forest maintains 12 canoe routes outside the Boundary Waters Canoe Area Wilderness (BWCA) that are similar in nature to the BWCA. Park rangers in the Voyageurs National Park can suggest numerous canoe routes that are close to shorelines in areas where islands give shelter from the wind. Remember that at Voyageurs National Park, the canoeists share the lakes with fishing boats, houseboats, runabouts, cabin cruisers, and sailboats.

To these canoeing opportunities, add the 1,200 mile of canoe routes located in the BWCA Wilderness and you realize that even for the avid canoeist, it's probably impossible to canoe each route in one's lifetime. What a challenge to try!

Also available from the Minnesota Office of Tourism is a new brochure/directory *Explore Minnesota Canoe Outfitters* that lists and describes 38 full-service outfitters for the BWCA Wilderness from the Ely, Grand Marais, and Crane Lake areas; Voyageurs National Park; Lake of the Woods; and the Crow Wing, Root and Mississippi rivers.

ST. CROIX NATIONAL SCENIC RIVERWAY

Since there are numerous primitive campsites on the Riverway, and camping opportunities at four Minnesota state parks and two state forests, as well as canoe rentals at four state parks, I decided to include highlights of the Minnesota section of the St. Croix National Scenic Waterway in this *Camper's Guide.*.

The St. Croix National Scenic Riverway, which includes the Namekagon River in Wisconsin, was established in 1968 as one of the original eight rivers under the National Wild and Scenic Rivers Act. The Lower St. Croix National Scenic Riverway was added to the system in 1972. Together they form a 252-mile riverway that offers outdoor enthusiasts a change to enjoy a wilderness-like experience and a variety of outdoor recreation opportunities. Free-flowing and unpolluted, the Namekagon and St. Croix Rivers flow through some of the most scenic and least developed country in the Upper Midwest. For canoeists, a variety of trips is possible, from leisurely afternoon excursions to week-long expeditions.

On the Upper St. Croix and Namekagon Rivers, rapids challenge the canoeist, although none of the Riverway's waters are classified as whitewater. At the lower end, where the river widens out as Lake St. Croix, power boats, large and small, sail boats, and even houseboats, are popular. The Riverway is managed through the cooperative efforts of the National Park Service, the Minnesota and Wisconsin Departments of Natural Resources, and the Northern States Power Company.

It is recommended that anyone planning a canoe trip on the St. Croix should obtain maps and other information prior to the trip. The National Park Service has a brochure/map on the St. Croix National Scenic Riverway as well as other handouts on campgrounds, canoe services, river section maps, etc. The Minnesota DNR has individual canoe route maps available on five river sections: Trego, Wisconsin to St. Croix State Park; St. Croix State Park to Highway 70; Highway 70 to Wild River State Park; Wild River State Park to William O'Brien State Park; and William O'Brien State Park to the Mississippi River.

River maps show the "0" mile marker at Prescott, Wisconsin where the St. Croix River joins the Mississippi River. With this reference point in

Minnesota's rivers and lakes are lined with enough canoe campsites to handle even a "water-borne war party" of this size.

mind, journey with me upriver to River Mile 141.5 where the St. Croix becomes the border between Wisconsin and Minnesota. Granted, there are other canoe access points along the river, but since this *Camper's Guide* is about campgrounds at state parks and state forests, often the basecamp for other outdoor activities, these specific areas are briefly highlighted.

St. Croix State Forest has a canoe access at Mile 124 according to the state forest map. A few miles farther down the river, the St. Croix State Park has 4 canoe access sites and 3 canoe campsites between River Mile 121 and 107, with a capacity of 100. The park also rents canoes and has a canoe shuttle service. Popular trips from the park include a trip, approximately 4 hours in time, from SH 48 (Mile 129), or an all-day trip from Riverside at Wisconsin Highway 35 (Mile 144) down river to the park. A shorter, 2-hour trip, is from the canoe rental area in the park to Sand Creek Landing (Mile 114), also in the park. Maps of the adjacent Chengwatana State Forest indicate 3 canoe campsites and 3 canoe access sites between Mile 95 and 89.

Wild River State Park is next on the trip downstream. There are 15 canoe campsites at 4 locations with 2 river access sites between Mile 79 and 66. This park has a canoe rental and shuttle service. A popular day trip from this state park is the 10-mile section from Sunrise River Landing (within the park, but upstream from the main campground area) down river to the main boat landing. The main boat landing at Wild River State Park is at Mile 67.5 and the next 10 miles of river are the Indianhead Flowage created by the 60-foot high St. Croix Falls hydroelectric dam. Most canoeists take out upstream of the flowage to avoid the slack water. If the slack water doesn't discourage you, remember that the dam at the falls requires a 1¼-mile portage to the Interstate Park.

Downstream of the dam (at Taylors Falls, MN) are the high cliffs of the Dalles, which formed as meltwaters from retreating glaciers cut a deep, vertical-walled gorge through bedrock. For about 2 miles here the St. Croix River, in places 70-100 feet deep, flows its fastest. The Dalles mostly lie within two state parks named Interstate: one in Minnesota and the other in Wisconsin. The Minnesota Interstate State Park has a boat landing at the "Pothole" scenic area as well as a canoe access and canoe rental with shuttle service at the lower end of the park (Mile 55). The most popular canoe trips from this park include the 7-mile trip (approximately 3 hours) to the National Parks Service Osceola Canoe Landing and the 17-mile trip to William O'Brien State Park (approximately 5 hours). Some canoeists take 2 days to make the longer trip in order to camp along the way.

William O'Brien State Park is the last state park along the St. Croix River that has a canoe launch or canoe campsites. Afton State Park is located at Mile 9, but has only a rest area; that park is designed for backpackers. William O'Brien State Park has one boat launch ramp and a canoe campground with a capacity for 50; reservations are required. They rent canoes and have a shuttle service, from River Mile 38. One of their popular trips is the 10-mile from the Osceola Landing upstream, or the longer 17-mile trip from Interstate State Park at Taylors Falls.

There are numerous primitive campsites on the Riverway. You should camp at these rather than create new ones. There are no special use, camping, or fire permits required for use of the federal portion of the Riverway. The state parks charge entrance and camp fees. Camping in the federally administered area is limited to 3 days at any one site and a maximum of 14 days per season. Remember to carry out whatever you carry in and do not bury trash. Respect the property rights of those along the Riverway and do not disturb them or their property in any way; some land is still private property. If you plan to fish, you should have either a Wisconsin or a Minnesota fishing license where the St. Croix River borders both states.

There are special water surface use regulations enforced on the river between Taylors Falls and the Mississippi River to improve safety conditions. River users should obtain a copy of these boating rules before getting on the water.

Anybody home? Sleeping late . . . or out for a stroll???

This has been a rather brief exposure to the St. Croix National Scenic Riverway, but perhaps it has whetted your appetite to obtain additional information and to plan a trip real soon. Why take someone else's word for it that the St. Croix River flows through some of the most scenic and least developed country in the Upper Midwest?

The Headquarters Visitor Center is located on the north end of St. Croix Falls, Wisconsin, on the corner of Hamilton and Massachusetts Streets. This center is open seven days a week all year long except for holidays during the winter months. There are various exhibits located at this center, a 12-minute movie "St. Croix Reflections," and a 5-minute slide-sound program about the riverway, available for viewing upon request. The Visitor Center also has a variety of books, field guides, posters, postcards, etc. available for purchase.

There are two other visitor centers: one in Wisconsin on Highway 63 near Trego, and one on SH 70 on the Minnesota side of the St. Croix River about 5 miles west of Grantsburg, Wisconsin.

For Information:

National Park Service
St. Croix National Scenic Riverway
P.O. Box 708
St. Croix Falls, WI 54024
(715) 483-3284

BOUNDARY WATERS CANOE AREA WILDERNESS

The Boundary Waters Canoe Area Wilderness (BWCA) is unique in the National Wilderness Preservation System—it is the only lakeland wilderness in the country. Located in the Superior National Forest, it is over 1 million acres in size and extends

nearly 150 miles along the Canadian border adjacent to the Quetico Provincial Park. These unspoiled lands and waters make up the greatest canoeing and fishing area in the world. It contains several thousand portage-linked lakes and streams, interspersed with islands, woods, and crags. With 1,500 miles of water routes, the BWCA attracts thousands of visitors each year to canoe, portage, and camp in the spirit of the French Voyageurs of 200 years ago.

What is wilderness? It's an area of undeveloped land where man is a visitor who does not remain, where outstanding opportunities for solitude exist, and where the area is large enough to warrant preservation and use in an unspoiled, natural condition. If camping in the wilderness is your "thing" and you haven't been among the some 160,000 that visit the BWCA yearly, then this brief overview of the BWCA is definitely for you. Wilderness camping is quite different from the camping done at the developed campgrounds in Minnesota on which this *Camper's Guide* is focused. But, since the BWCA is such a unique area, highlights are included in this guide to present the recreational user with pertinent information regarding what to expect, what one should know, quotas and permits, where to make reservations, and where to obtain additional information.

To help preserve the BWCA's wilderness character, visitors are asked to observe BWCA regulations to help keep the area a place in which to have an outstanding recreational experience. The *BWCA Wilderness Visitor Information* brochure is available from the office of the Forest Supervisor of the Superior National Forest. The brochure has a map showing the names and locations of the 83 wilderness entrance points, a BWCA Reservation Appli-

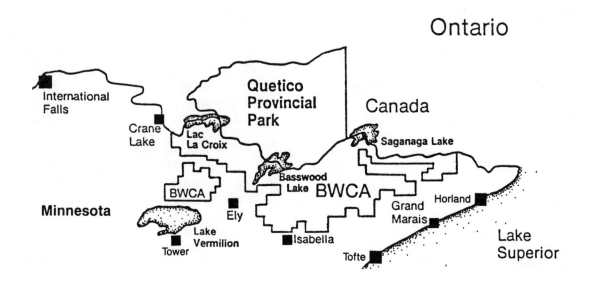

cation, and other information pertinent to users of the BWCA. Highlights of that brochure, as they pertain mainly to the canoeist, are cited here.

General Information

▲ Party size is limited to 10 persons or less.

▲ Camping, during the ice free season, is permitted only at developed Forest Service campsites having steel firegrates and wilderness latrines.

▲ Open campfires, during the ice-free season, are permitted only within the steel firegrates at developed campsites. Leave your axe at home; there is an abundance of dead wood.

▲ Containers of fuel, insect repellant, medicines, personal toilet articles, and other items which are not foods or beverages are the only cans and bottles you may bring.

▲ All empty containers and other refuse must be burned or packed out. Pack a bag to carry out litter found along your route or at the campsites. Leave the campsite as you found it or in even better condition.

▲ You must know how to use a compass and read a map; you will be on your own in an unfamiliar environment.

▲ You must be prepared to meet the unexpected, such as accidents, illness, rainy weather, and high winds on the larger lakes.

▲ You may bring dogs into the BWCA; keep them on a leash while on portages and prevent excessive barking.

▲ Outboard motor use is not allowed on most lakes and motor size is restricted on lakes where motors are allowed. Inquire as to all rules pertaining to the use of motors.

▲ The state of Minnesota requires licensing of all watercraft used in the state. A Minnesota license is not required for watercraft legally licensed in other states.

▲ If you plan to fish in the Superior National Forest, you must have a fishing license.

▲ Make sure you have a current year map showing campsite locations. Canoe route maps that have been reviewed by the Forest Service for accuracy are available from:
W. A. Fisher Company
Virginia, MN 55792
and
McKenzie Maps
727 Board of Trade Bldg.
Duluth, MN 55802
These maps are also available from outfitters at communities adjacent to the BWCA.

▲ A 15-minute slide tape program titled "Are You Wilderness Wise" is available for groups to use in preparing for their BWCA trip. To borrow a copy write to the Forest Supervisor, P. O. Box 338, Duluth, MN 55801.

▲ For information about the BWCA, contact one of the Ranger District offices nearest your selected entry point. They have the most current information on water levels, campsite conditions, etc. Refer to the Superior National Forest Map in Region II of this *Camper's Guide* to view the Ranger district boundaries and obtain the phone numbers.

Quotas, Permits and Reservations

▲ Entry quotas have been established for overnight campers in order to reduce competition for the limited number of established campsites and avoid unauthorized camping on undeveloped sites.

▲ A visitor's permit must be obtained before entering the BWCA from May 1 through September 30 for any overnight trip, regardless of mode of travel. A permit is not required for paddle or hiking day trips.

▲ A permit may be obtained free of charge from any Superior National Forest office or cooperating business (outfitter, resort, camp, etc.) as early as 48 hours ahead of the planned trip.

▲ The permit may only be used by the party leader or alternate—they are not transferable. Identification is required and will be asked for during periodic checks at landings and in the BWCA.

▲ A permit will allow a party of up to 10 people to enter the BWCA only on the day and through the entrance point specified on the permit. Once in the wildnerness, a party is free to travel where they desire.

▲ The major BWCA entry points are near Crane Lake, Ely, Grand Marais, and Tofte. Access is also possible from Tower and from the Arrowhead Trail north of Hovland.

▲ People who plan ahead, make reservations, and are somwhat flexible in their starting date and entry point should have little trouble getting into the BWCA.

▲ There are 83 entry points to the BWCA. During the heavy use periods, you may want to begin your trip at an entry point that receives less use.

▲ A reservation is recommended if you plan to visit during heavy use periods. A reservation assures that a permit to enter the BWCA on a specific day and at a certain entry point will be available.

▲ A $5.00 nonrefundable fee is charged for the reservation service and is required for each overnight trip for which a reservation is made. Any change will be considered a new reservation and will require a new service fee.

▲ All reservations, regardless of the desired entrance point, are made through a central reservation office. *This office only processes reservations and is not equipped to handle any type of information calls.* Mail requests for reservations will be accepted beginning February 1 at the following address:

BWCA Reservations
Superior National Forest
P. O. Box 338
Duluth, MN 55801

Phone reservations will also be accepted beginning February 1 with the use of a valid VISA/Mastercard at the following number: (218) 720-5440.

Canada's Quetico Provincial Park

Visitors to the Quetico Provincial Park in Canada are subject to rules similar to those for the BWCA. U.S. citizens must clear Canadian Customs and immigration before reporting to the Quetico Ranger Station when entering the canoe park. Entry permits are limited and may be reserved. For information concerning permit reservations and Quetico Park rules, write:

District Manager
Ministry of Natural Resources
Atikokan, Ontario POT ICO
(807) 597-2735

Backcountry Ethics

Rules imposed by those who administer the various trails are common sense rules meant to control actions that may damage natural resources. In recent years, the term "going light" has taken on new meaning. To a backpacker, "going light" is the skill of paring down the load and leaving at home every ounce that can be spared. But "going light" also means to spare the land and travel and camp by the rules of "low impact." The National Forest Service suggests the following "low-impact" rules. Although these suggestions were written for the hiker and backpacker, they are quite appropriate for anyone using the backcountry, whether they are traveling by foot, canoe, bicycle, or horse.

General Information

1. Don't short-cut trails. Trails are designed and maintained to prevent erosion.
2. Cutting across switchbanks and trampling meadows can create a confusing maze of unsightly trails.
3. Don't pick flowers, dig up plants, or cut branches from live trees. Leave them for others to see and enjoy.

Plan Your Trip

1. Keep your party small.
2. Take a gas stove to help conserve firewood.
3. Bring sacks to carry out your trash.
4. Take a light shovel or trowel to help with personal sanitation.
5. Carry a light basin or collapsible bucket for washing.

One of the most interesting geologic features in the Temperance River State Park (page 100) is the narrow gorge with its many waterfalls. The 3,400-acre George H. Crosby-Manitou State Park (page 72) is nearby; it offers camping in isolated backpacking sites along the Manitou River. Camp by the rules of "low impact" (see "Backcountry Ethics," page 25).

6. Check on weather conditions and water availability.
7. Before your hike, study maps of the area, get permits if necessary, and learn the terrain.

Setting Up Camp
1. Pick a campsite where you won't need to clear away vegetation or level a tent site.
2. Use an existing campsite, if available.
3. Camp 300 feet from streams or springs. Law prohibits camping within 1/4 mile of an only available water source (for wildlife or livestock).
4. Do not cut trees, limbs or brush to make camp improvements. Carry own tent poles.

Breaking Camp
1. Before leaving camp, naturalize the area. Replace rocks and wood used; scatter needles, leaves, and twigs on the campsite.
2. Scout the area to be sure you've left nothing behind. Everything you packed into your camp should be packed out. Try to make it appear as if no one had been there.

Campfires
1. Use gas stoves when possible to conserve dwindling supplies of firewood.
2. If you need to build a fire, use an existing campfire site. Keep it small. Before you leave, make sure it is out.
3. If you need to clear a new fire site, select a safe spot away from rock ledges that would be blackened by smoke; away from meadows where it would destroy grass and leave a scar; away from dense brush, trees and duff, where it would be a fire hazard.
4. Clear a circle of all burnable materials. Dig a shallow pit for the fires. Keep the sod intact.
5. Use only fallen timber for firewood. Even standing dead trees are part of the beauty of wilderness, and are important to wildlife.
6. Put your fire cold out before leaving, let the fire burn down to ashes, mix the ashes with dirt and water. Feel it with your hand. If it's cold out, cover the ashes in the pit with dirt, replace the sod, naturalize the disturbed area. Rockfire rings, if needed or used, should be scattered before leaving.

Pack It In—Pack It Out
1. Bring trash bags to carry out all trash that cannot be completely burned.
2. Aluminum foil and aluminum lined packages won't burn up in your fire. Compact it and put it in your trash bag.
3. Cigarette butts, pull-tags, and gum wrappers are litter, too. They can spoil a campsite and trail.
4. Don't bury trash! Animals dig it up.
5. Try to pack out trash left by others. Your good example may catch on!

Keep The Water Supply Clean
1. Wash yourself, your dishes, and your clothes in a container.
2. Pour wash water on the ground away from streams and springs
3. Food scraps, tooth paste, even biodegradable soap will pollute streams and springs. Remember, it's your drinking water, too!
4. Boil water or treat water before drinking it.

Disposing of Human Waste
1. When nature calls, select a suitable spot at least 100 feet from open water, campsites, and trails. Dig a hole 4 to 6 inches deep. Try to keep the sod intact.
2. After use, fill in the hole completely burying waste. Then tramp in the sod.

Emergency Items
1. According to conditions, carry extra warm clothing such as windbreakers, wool jackets, hats, and gloves. Keep extra high-energy foods like hard candies, chocolate, dried fruits, or liquids accessible. Don't overload yourself, but be prepared for emergencies.
2. Travel with a first aid kit, map, compass, and whistle. Know how to use them.
3. Always leave your trip plan with a member of your family or a close friend.
4. Mishaps are rare, but they do happen. Should one occur, remain calm. In case of an accident, someone should stay with the injured person. Notify the nearest state, local, or federal law enforcement office for aid.

See Appendix on page 142 for a hiking/backpacking checklist.

Region 1

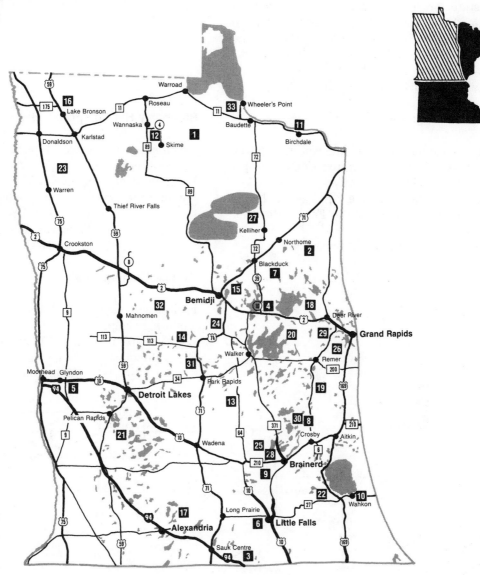

1—Beltrami Island State Forest, 28
2—Big Fork State Forest, 63
3—Birch Lake State Forest, 63
4—Bowstring State Forest, 63
5—Buffalo River State Park, 29
6—Charles A. Lindbergh State Park, 29
7—Chippewa National Forest, 31–37
8—Crow Wing State Forest, 38
9—Crow Wing State Park, 39
10—Father Hennepin State Park, 40
11—Franz Jevne State Park, 41
12—Hayes Lake State Park, 42
13—Huntersville State Forest, 43
14—Itasca State Park, 44–45
15—Lake Bemidji State Park, 46
16—Lake Bronson State Park, 47
17—Lake Carlos State Park, 48

18—Lake Winnibigoshish Recreation Area, 49
19—Land O'Lakes State Forest, 50
20—Leech Lake Recreation Area, 51
21—Maplewood State Park, 52
22—Mille Lacs Kathio State Park, 53
23—Old Mill State Park, 54
24—Paul Bunyan State Forest, 55
25—Pillsbury State Forest, 56
26—Pokegama Lake Recreation Area, 57
27—Red Lake State Forest, 63
28—Ronald Louis Cloutier Recreation Area, 58
29—Schoolcraft State Park, 59
30—Terry R. Johnson Recreation Area, 60
31—Two Inlets State Forest, 61
32—White Earth State Forest, 63
33—Zippel Bay State Park, 62

Beltrami Island State Forest

This state forest, the second largest of Minnesota's 56 state forests, contains more than 669,000 acres of land. Recreational facilities on the forest include 3 state forest campgrounds, Hayes Lake State Park, and the 76-mile Beltrami Island Snowmobile Trail that connects with the 52.5-mile Baudette/Norris Snowmobile Trail.

Bemis Hill Campground

Facilities—4 campsites, drinking water, 6 picnic sites, shelter, horse corral, winter sledding slope, and access to snowmobile trails.

Location—from Warroad take CR 5 south for 12 miles, turn west on Thompson Forest Road for 6¼ miles.

For Information—Area Forest Supervisor
Box 43
Warroad, MN 56763
(218) 386-1304

Blueberry Hill Campground

Facilities—8 campsites, 4 picnic sites, blueberry picking in season.

Location—from Williams, 4 miles west on SH 11.

For Information—Area Forest Supervisor
Rt. 1, Box 1001
Baudette, MN 56623
(218) 634-2172

Faunce Campground

Facilities—6 campsites, 2 picnic sites, wooded site, hunting camp.

Location—from Williams, 12 miles south on CR 2.

For Information—(same as for Blueberry Hill Campground)

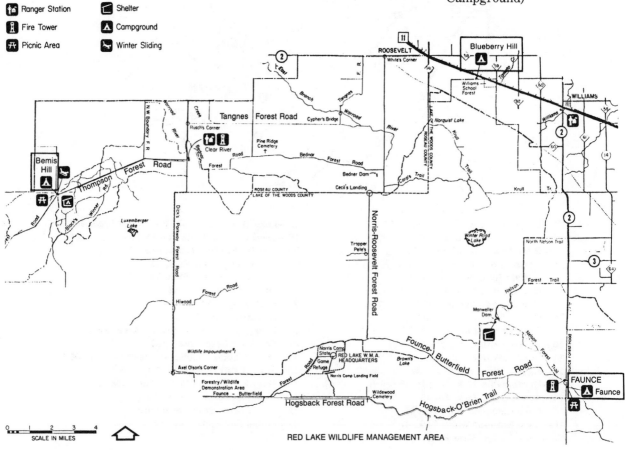

Buffalo River State Park

For Information

Buffalo River State Park
Rt. 2, Box 118
Glyndon, MN 56547
(218) 498-2124

Location

Buffalo River State Park is located in Clay County 4.5 miles east of Glyndon or 13 miles east of Moorhead. Entrance to the 1,240-acre park is from U.S. 10. The first explorers in the Red River Valley encountered a sea of grass stretching to the horizon, interrupted only by meandering river-bottom forests. Buffalo River State Park preserves a remnant of that early landscape—both prairie and woods. The Buffalo River bisects the park and is bordered by riverbottom forest of elm, ash, cottonwood, oak, and basswood.

Facilities & Activities

44 drive-in campsites
8 campsites with electricity
dump station
flush toilets (H)
showers (H)
rustic group camp
picnic area (H)
swimming
fishing (stream)
visitor center (seasonal)
interpretive program (seasonal)
winter access
12 miles of foot trails
.6 mile of self-guided trails
12 miles of X-country ski trails

❓ Information		🏊 Swimming Pool	
⛱ Picnic Area		🚻 Trailer Sanitation Station	
⛺ Campground		👥 Primitive Group Camp	
🔱 Interpretive Center		········ Hiking	

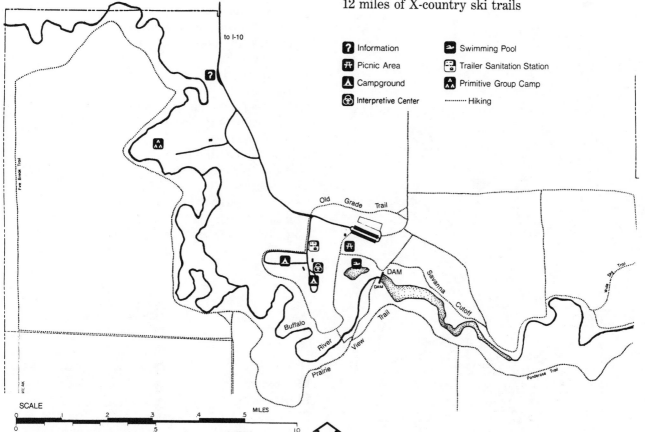

Charles A. Lindbergh State Park

For Information

Charles A. Lindbergh State Park
P.O. Box 364
Little Falls, MN 56345
(612) 632-9050

Location

Charles A. Lindbergh State Park is located in Morrison County, 2 miles south of Little Falls along the Mississippi River. The park entrance is off of Lindbergh Drive (County Road 52). The picturesque Pike Creek meanders through the center of the 328-acre park and empties into the Mississippi River in the southern part of the park.

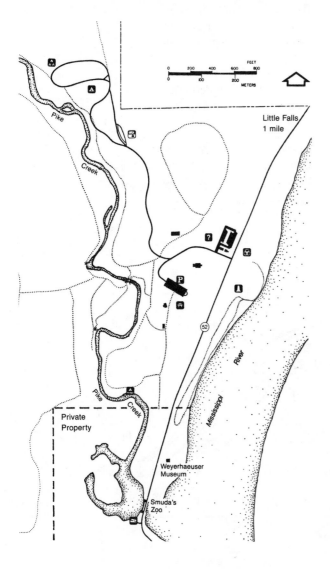

About the Park

Charles A. Lindbergh, Jr., world renowned for his trans-Atlantic solo flight in 1927, lived his boyhood years in the gray 1½-story house overlooking the Mississippi River. The house was built in 1906 by Lindbergh's father, Charles, Sr., the park's namesake. The Lindbergh House is administered by the Minnesota Historical Society, which recently restored the house as closely as possible to its 1907–1917 appearance. The Historical Society also constructed a visitor's center nearby to tell the story of the Lindbergh family.

Facilities & Activities

38 drive-in campsites
2 canoe campsites on Pine Creek
dump station
flush toilets (H)
vault toilets (H)
showers (H)
rustic group camp (50 capacity)
picnic area with enclosed shelter
fishing (river)
boat launch on Mississippi
visitor center (year-round)
winter access
historic site—Lindbergh House
6 miles of foot trails
5.5 miles of X-country ski trails

TRAILS
······· Hiking
＊ Overlook

FACILITIES
Information
Picnic Area
Campground
Trailer Sanitation Station

Historic Site / Lindbergh Boyhood Home
Interpretive Center
Parking
Canoe Camping (2 sites)
Group Camp
Boat Ramp
PRIVATE PROPERTY
Public Use Prohibited

Chippewa National Forest

For Information

Supervisor's Office
Chippewa National Forest
Route 3, Box 244
Cass Lake, MN 56633
(218) 335-2226

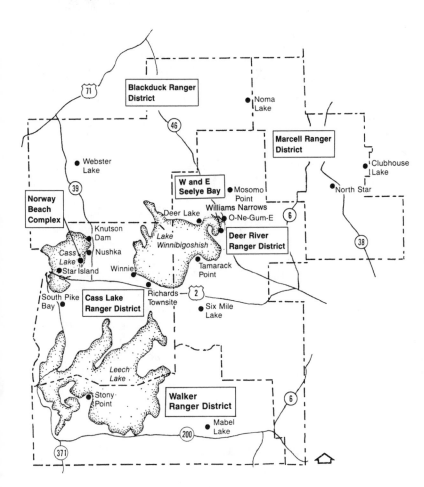

Schoolcraft State Park (page 59), located within the boundaries of the Chippewa National Forest, contains 295 acres, much of which is virgin pine timber. This tree is the park's pride-and-joy!

About the Forest

Established in 1908, the Chippewa National Forest was the first national forest east of the Mississippi River. Originally known as the Minnesota National Forest, the name was changed in 1928 to honor the original inhabitants.

The forest boundary encompasses about 1.6 million acres, with about 660,000 acres managed by the Chippewa National Forest. The remaining lands are state, county, Indian, and private. The Leech Lake Indian Reservation is also within the forest boundary.

The forest boasts of being home to the largest breeding population of bald eagles in the lower 48 states. The Chippewa's Forest Plan aims for 150 active breeding pairs on the Forest; in 1987 there were 125 pairs. Eagles are often viewed soaring over the larger lakes of the area. Several sensitive species such as the osprey, loon, and great gray owl also make the Chippewa their home.

Water is abundant on the Chippewa, with over 700 lakes, 920 miles of streams, and 150,000 acres of wetlands. The forest's landscape is a reminder of the glaciers which blanketed northern Minnesota some 10,000 years ago. Due to the large number of lakes, water-oriented recreation such as fishing, canoeing, camping, water-skiing and swimming are popular on the Chippewa.

Twenty-four developed campgrounds are located on the major lakes. Campgrounds are generally open from mid-May to mid-September; some are open year-long with no water or garbage pickup off-season. Campground facilities vary from flush toilets and showers to rustic campgrounds with vault toilets and handpump. Each campsite has a picnic table, fireplace, tent pad, and parking spot.

If you are seeking a more primitive experience, there are over 400 dispersed recreation sites in the forest; these sites are free of charge, have limited facilities, and allow you to "get away from it all." Visitors are not limited to camping at designated areas only. Campers are free to camp anywhere on national forest land unless otherwise posted. Don't forget that if you "pack it in, pack it out" leaving the area as you would like to find it.

Over 160 miles of trail offer the opportunity to view the forest up close. Information on 25 trails is displayed in a flyer entitled *Hiking*, available from any of the district ranger stations or from the forest headquarters. Several primitive campsites are located along the trail routes. In the winter, these trails mean X-country skiing, snowshoeing, and snowmobiling.

The Chippewa National Forest offers 9 canoe routes, ranging from the mighty Mississippi and the unpredictable Leech Lake to the slow-moving Shingobee River and small creeks. These are not wilderness trips; however, most are lightly traveled. Extreme caution should be used in crossing the larger lakes. Primitive campsites are located along most of the rivers. Information on the 9 canoe routes is displayed in a flyer entitled *Canoeing*, available from any of the district ranger stations or from the forest headquarters.

Cut Foot Sioux Visitor Information Center is located on State Highway 46, about 17 miles northwest of Deer River. The center is open daily 10 a.m. to 5 p.m. and Wednesdays until 9 p.m. during the summer. The center offers visitors information, displays, films, a bookstore, and Wednesday's evening programs. Cut Foot Sioux gets its name after the last battle between the Chippewa and Sioux Indians in 1748.

The Chippewa National Forest Supervisor's Office is located in Cass Lake in a three-story log building constructed in the 1930's by the Civilian Conservation Corps. It is listed in the National Register of Historic Places. The building, containing 8,500 square feet of floor space and more than 16,000 lineal feet of red pine logs, is believed to be one of the largest log buildings in existence.

Also of interest to the forest visitor is a flyer entitled *Unique Areas*, that describes 12 "special places" and 6 areas of "geologic interest" to visit within the forest. Pick up a copy so you, too, can visit these unique areas in the Chippewa National Forest.

Blackduck Ranger District

For Information

Blackduck Ranger District
Chippewa National Forest
Blackduck, MN 56630
(218) 835-4291

Campground Locations

Noma Lake Campground—On Noma Lake; 1.8 miles northwest of Wirt on CR 31

Webster Lake Campground—On Webster Lake; 7.1 miles south from Blackduck on CR 39, 1 mile east on FR 2207, 2 miles south on FR 2236

Most campsites have a parking spur to accommodate trailers.

Campgrounds	Camping Units*	Toilets**	Showers	Dump Station	Picnic Area	Boat Ramp	Swimming Site
Noma Lake	14	V			X		
Webster Lake	22*	V			X	X	

Notes:
Noma Lake is open year-long with reduced services.
 * Accessible to the handicapped.
 ** V = vault, F = flush

Cass Lake Ranger District

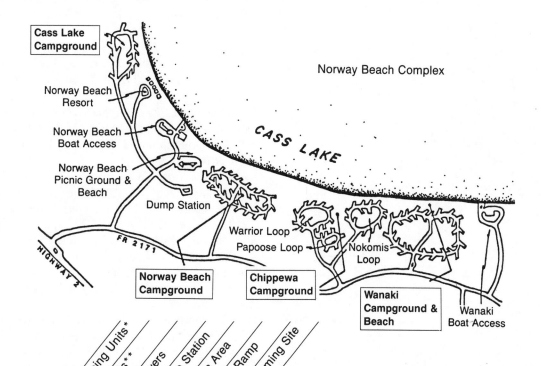

Campgrounds	Camping Units*	Toilets**	Showers	Dump Station	Picnic Area	Boat Ramp	Swimming Site
Cass Lake	21	F	X	X	X	X	X
Chippewa	46*	F	X	X	X	X	X
Norway Beach	55	F		X	X	X	X
Wanaki	46	F	X	X	X	X	X
Knutson Dam	14	V				X	
Nushka Group Site	20	V			X		
Richards Town Site	7	V				X	
South Pike Bay	21	V			X	X	X
Star Island	3	V					
Winnie	42	V			X	X	

Notes:
Cass Lake, Knutson Dam, Richards Town Site, South Pike Bay, Star Island, and Winnie campsites are open year-long with reduced services.
 * Accessible to the handicapped.
** V = vault, F = flush

The common loon is the state bird of Minnesota. Canoeists traveling the wilderness waterways thrill to the "call of the Loon" . . . a bird call you'll never forget!

For Information

Cass Lake Ranger District
Chippewa National Forest
Route 3, Box 219
Cass Lake, MN 56633
(218) 335-2283

Campground Locations

Norway Beach Complex (Cass Lake, Chippewa, Norway Beach, and Wanaki Campgrounds)—On Cass Lake; 4.2 miles east from the city of Cass Lake on U.S. 2, then less than 3 miles north on FR 2171 to the 4 campground-complex.

Chippewa National Forest *(continued)*

Knutson Dam Recreation Area

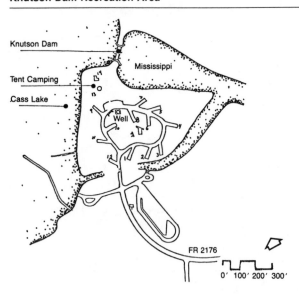

Knutson Dam Campground—On Cass Lake; 6 miles east from the city of Cass Lake on U.S. 2, 5.3 miles north on CR 10, .7 mile west on FR 2176.

Nushka Group Site Campground—On Cass Lake; 6 miles east from the city of Cass Lake on U.S. 2, 4.5 miles north on CR 10, 1.2 miles northwest on FR 2360.

Richards Town Site Campground—On Lake Winnibigoshish; 2.8 miles northwest from Bena on U.S. 2, .3 mile north on FR 2167, .1 mile northeast on FR 2074.

South Pike Bay Campground—On Pike Bay; 3 miles south from the city of Cass Lake on SH 371, .7 mile east on CR 146, 1.3 miles southeast on FR 2137, .3 mile north on FR 2137A.

Star Island Campground—On Star Island in Cass Lake, access by boat; boat ramp nearest the island is 1 mile north from the city of Cass Lake on CR 60, then approximately 1 mile north and east on CR 148.

Winnie Campground—On Lake Winnibigoshish; 6 miles east from the city of Cass Lake on U.S. 2, 2.3 miles north on CR 10, 7.1 miles northeast on FR 2171, 3.5 miles southeast on FR 2168.

Nushka
Group Camping

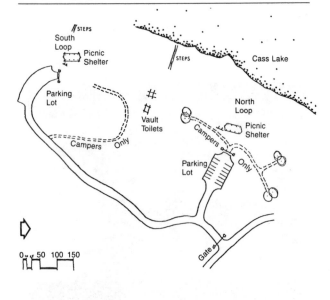

Winnie Recreation Area

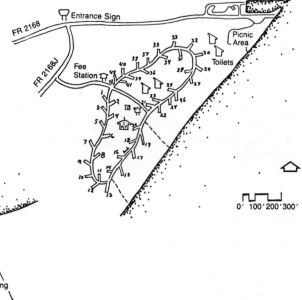

Pike Bay

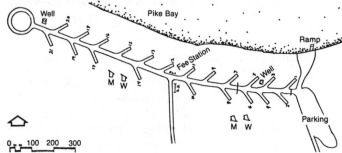

Deer River Ranger District

Campgrounds	Camping Units*	Toilets**	Showers	Dump Station	Picnic Area	Boat Ramp	Swimming Site
Deer Lake	48	V				X	X
East Seelye Bay	13	V			X	X	X
Mosomo Point	23	V				X	
O-Ne-Gum-E	46*	V				X	
Six Mile Lake	11	V				X	
Tamarack Point	35	V				X	
West Seelye Bay	22	V				X	
Williams Narrows	17	V			X	X	X

Notes:
Deer Lake, Mosomo Point, and Tamarack Point are open
  year-long with reduced services.
  * Accessible to the handicapped.
** V = vault, F = flush

For Information

Deer River Ranger District
Chippewa National Forest
Box 308
Deer River, MN 56636
(218) 246-2123

Campground Locations

Deer Lake Campground—On Cut Foot Sioux Lake;
1 mile northwest from Deer River on U.S. 2, 19.3
miles northwest on SH 46, 3 miles southwest on
CR 33, .9 mile south on FR 3153.

East Seelye Bay Campground—On East Seelye
Bay of Cut Foot Sioux Lake; 1 mile northwest
from Deer River on U.S. 2, 19.3 miles northwest
on SH 46, 2.5 miles southwest on CR 33.

Mosomo Point Campground—1 mile northwest
from Deer River on U.S. 2, 18.2 miles northwest
on SH 46, .6 mile southwest on FR 2190.

O-Ne-Gum-E Campground—1 mile northwest from
Deer River on U.S. 2, 18 miles northwest on SH
46, .1 mile east on FR 2507.

Six Mile Lake Campground—On Six Mile Lake; 1.5
miles east from Bena on U.S. 2, 3.8 miles southeast on FR 2127.

Tamarack Point Campground—On Lake Winnibigoshish; 1.5 miles east from U.S. 2, 5.6 miles
northeast on CR 9, 3.5 miles northwest on FR
2163.

West Seelye Bay Campground—On West Seelye
Bay off Cut Foot Sioux Lake; 1 mile northwest
from Deer River on U.S. 2, 19.3 miles northwest
on SH 46, 3 miles southwest on CR 33, 1 mile
south on FR 3153.

Williams Narrows Campground—On Cut Foot
Sioux Lake; 1 mile northwest from Deer River on
U.S. 2, 15.1 miles northwest on SH 46, 2 miles
northwest on CR 148.

Snowmobiling is a popular winter activity. There are 11,600 miles of marked and groomed snowmobile trails in Minnesota. More than 160 miles of these trails are available in the Chippewa National Forest. Many would say it's the only way to see Minnesota outdoors when snow covers the land.

Marcell Ranger District

For Information

Marcell Ranger District
Chippewa National Forest
Box 127
Marcell, MN 56657
(218) 832-3161

Campground Locations

Clubhouse Lake Campground—on Clubhouse Lake; .5 mile north from Marcell on SH 38, 5 miles east on CR 45, 1.2 miles north on FR 2181, 1.2 miles east on FR 3758.

North Star Campground—on North Star Lake; 3.5 miles southeast of Marcell on SH 38.

Campgrounds	Camping Units*	Toilets**	Showers	Dump Station	Picnic Area	Boat Ramp	Swimming Site
Clubhouse Lake	48*	V				X	X
North Star	21*	V				X	X

Notes:
Clubhouse Lake is open year-long with reduced services.
 * Accessible to the handicapped.
** V = vault, F = flush

The Bald Eagle, our National bird, is a frequent sight in many parts of Minnesota . . . if you look for it! It soars majestically, high in the air; its nest is a huge pile of sticks, added to each year, in a tall tree or high ledge. The young do not get white feathers on the head and tail until the fourth or fifth year, when they mature.

Chippewa National Forest *(continued)*

Walker Ranger District

Campgrounds	Camping Units*	Toilets**	Showers	Dump Station	Picnic Area	Boat Ramp	Swimming Site
Mabel Lake	22	V			X	X	X
Stony Point	45*	F		X	X	X	X

Notes:
Stony Point is open year-long with reduced services.
 * Accessible to the handicapped.
** V = vault, F = flush

Stony Point Campground

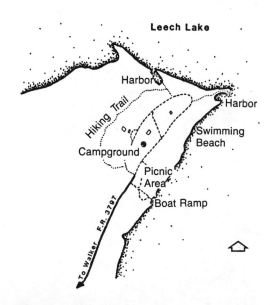

Mabel Lake Campground

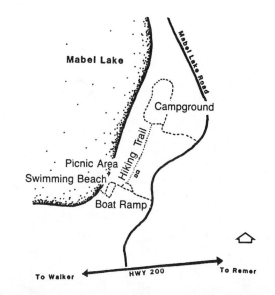

Campground Locations

Mabel Lake Campground—on Mabel Lake; 7.4 miles west from Remer on SH 200, .3 mile north on FR 2104.

Stony Point Campground—on Leech Lake; from Walker, 4 miles southeast on SH 371, 1.8 miles east on SH 200, 4.4 miles north on CR 13, 4.8 miles northeast on FR 3797.

For Information

Walker Ranger District
Chippewa National Forest
HCR 73, Box 15
Walker, MN 56484
(218) 547-1044

These boaters have just returned from a pleasure cruise on Leech Lake. They seem to want to linger a little longer.

Crow Wing State Forest
(Greer Lake Campground)

For Information

Area Forest Supervisor
1601 Minnesota Drive
Brainerd, MN 56401
(218) 828-2565

Facilities

34 campsites	swimming
fee area	water access
drinking water	fishing
2 picnic sites	nature trail

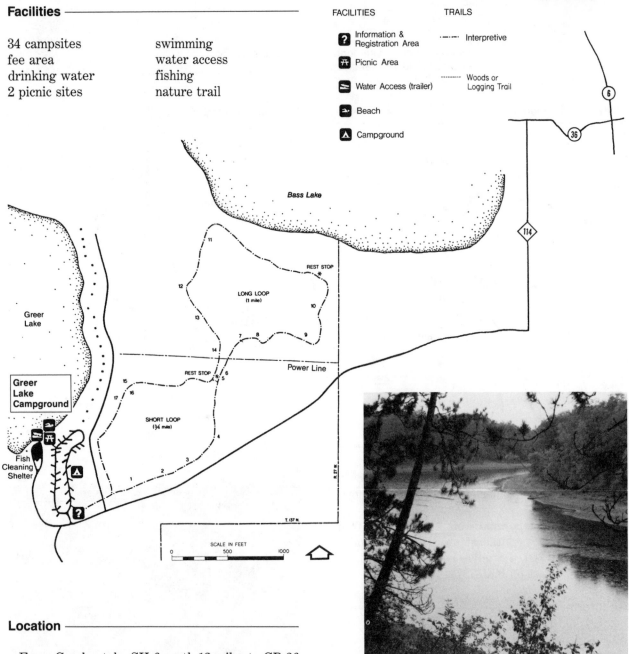

FACILITIES

? Information & Registration Area

🏕 Picnic Area

Water Access (trailer)

Beach

Campground

TRAILS

Interpretive

Woods or Logging Trail

Bass Lake

REST STOP

LONG LOOP
(1 mile)

Greer Lake

Power Line

REST STOP

Greer Lake Campground

SHORT LOOP
(¾ mile)

Fish Cleaning Shelter

SCALE IN FEET
0   500   1000

The Mississippi River winds its way through Crow Wing State Forest and Crow Wing State Park. Canoe camping is allowed.

Location

From Crosby, take SH 6 north 12 miles to CR 36 and turn left (west); then 3 miles to CR 114 and turn left (south), travel 1.5 miles and turn right (west), follow signs for 2 miles.

Crow Wing State Park

For Information

Crow Wing State Park
7100 State Park Road, S.W.
Brainerd, MN 56401
(218) 829-8022

Location

Crow Wing State Park is located 9 miles south of Brainerd on State Highway 371, then 1 mile west via Crow Wing County Road 27. The 2,042-acre park is located at the confluence of the Mississippi and Crow Wing Rivers. Here was the scene of a major battle between the Sioux and the Chippewa in 1868. A trading post was established along the south mouth of the Crow Wing River in 1823 and mission churches were later built. The park's historic site commemorates the old Crow Wing town site.

The displays in the outdoor interpretive center at Crow Wing State Park are of obvious interest to this park visitor.

Facilities & Activities

61 drive-in campsites
12 campsites with electricity
1 canoe campsite (50 capacity)
dump station
flush toilets (H)
vault toilets (H)
showers (H)
picnic area with enclosed shelter (H)
fishing (rivers)
boat launch
boat & canoe rental
information center (year-round)
interpretive program (seasonal)
winter access
historic site
14 miles of foot trails
6.4 miles of X-country ski trails
11.5 miles of snowmobile trails

FACILITIES

?	Information		Amphitheater
	Boat Landing		Historical Interpretive Center
	Picnic Area		Historic Site
	Campground		TRAILS
	Canoe Camping	......	Hiking

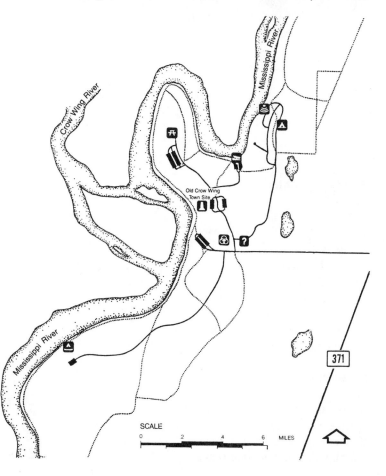

Father Hennepin State Park

For Information

Father Hennepin State Park
Box 397
Isle, MN 56342
(612) 676-8763

Location

Father Hennepin State Park is located in Mille Lacs County on the southeast shore of Mille Lacs Lake, the second largest freshwater lake entirely within Minnesota. The park is 1 mile northwest of Isle or 3 miles northeast of Wahkon on County Road 29 off of State Highway 27. This 316-acre park was named after Father Lewis Hennepin, a French Jesuit priest, who was the first recorded European explorer to visit the region now called Minnesota. His visit to this region occurred in 1679 and 1680.

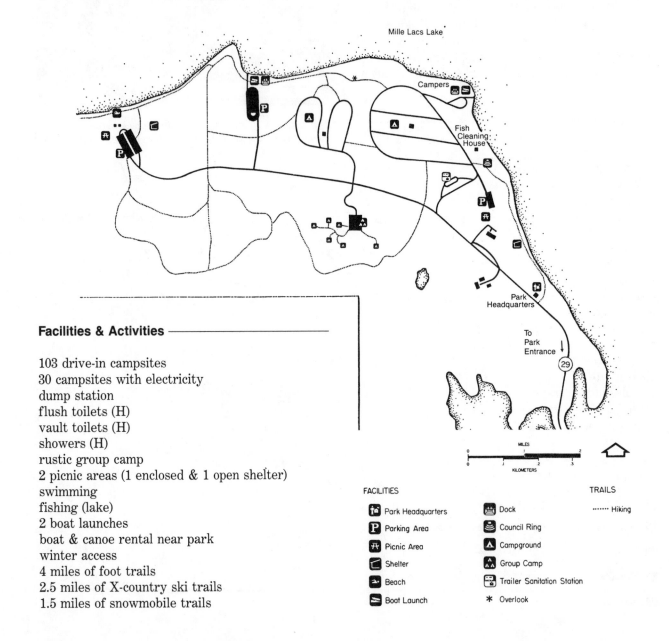

Facilities & Activities

103 drive-in campsites
30 campsites with electricity
dump station
flush toilets (H)
vault toilets (H)
showers (H)
rustic group camp
2 picnic areas (1 enclosed & 1 open shelter)
swimming
fishing (lake)
2 boat launches
boat & canoe rental near park
winter access
4 miles of foot trails
2.5 miles of X-country ski trails
1.5 miles of snowmobile trails

FACILITIES

🏠 Park Headquarters
P Parking Area
🪧 Picnic Area
▱ Shelter
⚓ Beach
⛴ Boat Launch

🛥 Dock
♨ Council Ring
△ Campground
⛺ Group Camp
🚐 Trailer Sanitation Station
✳ Overlook

TRAILS

······· Hiking

Franz Jevne State Park

For Information

Franz Jevne State Park
Rt. 3, Box 201
Birchdale, MN 56629
(no telephone)

Location

Franz Jevne State Park is located 2 miles east of Birchdale on State Highway 11, then 1 mile north on Koochiching County Road 85. This 118-acre park is located on the south shore of Rainy River, a boundary between Canada and the United States, and is approximately 40 miles west of International Falls and 27 miles east of Baudette.

The park land was donated to the state by the Franz Jevne family in 1967 for use as a public recreation area. This scenic area stretches for a mile along the river and has a good view of Canada. The rapids near the picnic area are called the Sault (pronounced Sue) Rapids and are navigable, as is the entire river, which was at one time the path of the Voyageurs. Both the Big Fork River and the Little Fork River state canoe routes run into the Rainy River above the park.

Facilities & Activities

11 rustic campsites
hand pump well
vault toilets
picnic area
fishing (river)
boat launch
1 mile of foot trails

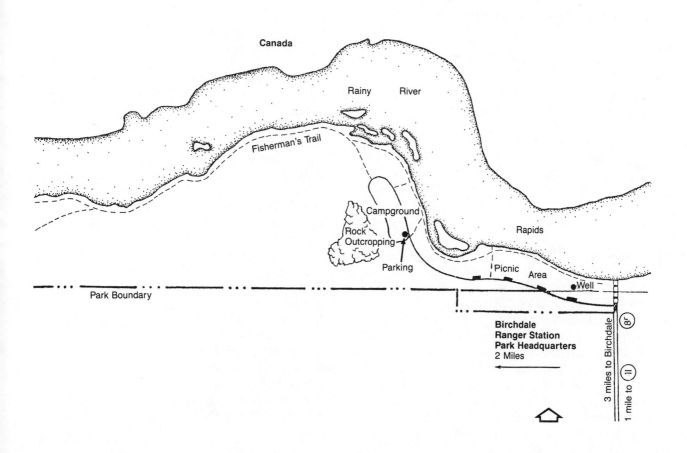

Hayes Lake State Park

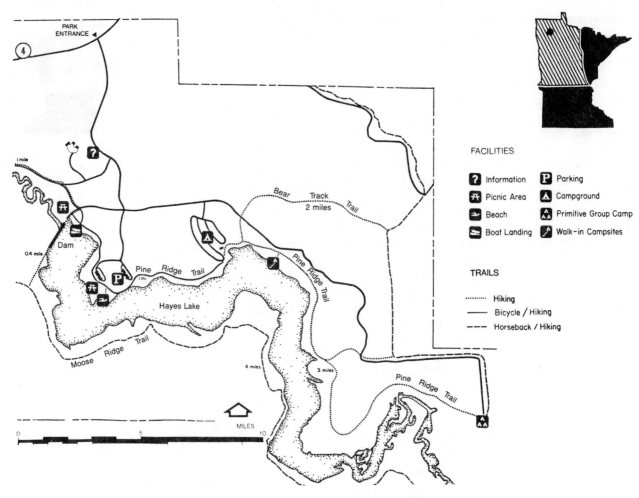

FACILITIES

? Information	P Parking
🅿 Picnic Area	⚠ Campground
🏖 Beach	Primitive Group Camp
Boat Landing	Walk-in Campsites

TRAILS

.... Hiking
——— Bicycle / Hiking
– – – Horseback / Hiking

For Information

Hayes Lake State Park
Star Route 4
Roseau, MN 56751
(218) 425-7504

Location

Hayes Lake State Park is located 22 miles southeast of Roseau on the north fork of the Roseau River. The park entrance is on Roseau County Road 4 approximately 7 miles east of State Highway 89. Because of the need for water-related recreation in the area, the initial development for the 2,950-acre park was the damming up of the river forming the lake, completed in 1973. The lake, the central focus to the park, and park were named in honor of Mr. A.F. Hayes, an early settler on the land now included in the park.

Facilities & Activities

35 drive-in campsites
2 walk-in campsites
flush toilets (H)
vault toilets (H)
showers (H)
horse camping
rustic group camp
picnic area
swimming
fishing (lake & river)
boat launch
interpretive program (seasonal)
winter access
boat motor restrictions
12 miles of foot trails
.5 mile of self-guided trails
3 miles of horseback riding trails
1 mile of bike trail
6 miles of X-country ski trails
6 miles of snowmobile trails

Huntersville State Forest

The Huntersville State Forest encompasses an area of 52 square miles. The major outdoor recreation facility in the forest is the Crow Wing River Canoe and Boating Route. There are 6 campsites at one location on the river, about 10 miles by river from Shell City Landing Campground. There are also 24 miles of groomed snowmobile/horseback riding trails, making the forest a year-round recreation facility.

For Information

Area Forest Supervisor
Backus, MN 56435
(218) 947-3232

Shell City Landing Campground

Facilities—18 campsites, fee area, drinking water, water access, fishing.

Location—Located on the Shell River that flows into the Crow Wing River. From Menahga, travel 4 miles east on CR 17, then left (north) for 1 mile on CR 23 to CR 18; turn right (east) and travel 3 miles to CR 24, turn left (north) for 1.2 miles.

Huntersville Forest Landing Campground

Facilities—13 campsites, fee area, drinking water, water access, fishing.

Location—Located on Crow Wing River. From Menahga, travel 4 miles east on CR 148, continue east for 3 miles on CR 150, continue east for 1.5 miles on forest road.

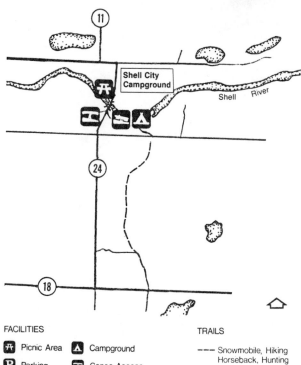

Shell City Campground

Shell River

FACILITIES

🅰 Picnic Area   🄰 Campground

🅿 Parking   ⬔ Canoe Access

🄲 Shelter   ⬓ Boat Access

TRAILS

––– Snowmobile, Hiking
Horseback, Hunting

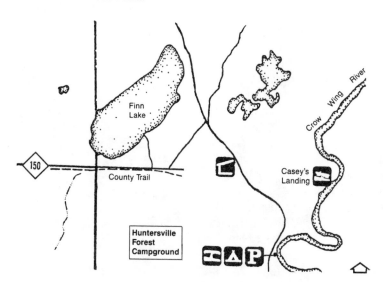

Finn Lake

150   County Trail

Casey's Landing

Crow Wing River

Huntersville Forest Campground

The 110-mile Crow Wing River Canoe & Boating Route that passes through Huntersville State Forest is one of 19 state canoe routes managed by the DNR (pages 19–21).

Itasca State Park

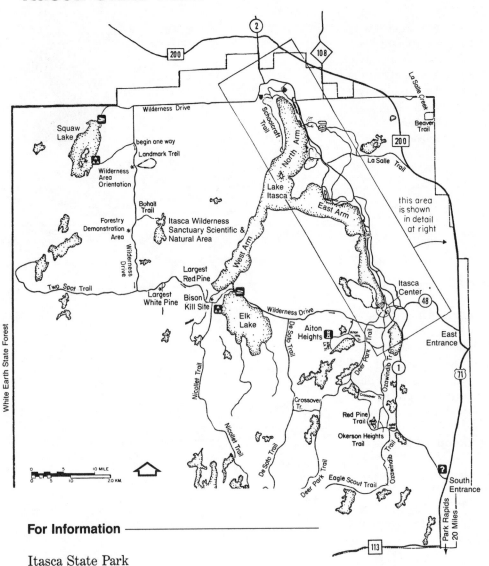

You're looking at the headwaters of the mighty Mississippi River. Young and old alike, cross over and back . . . a few wade, while others attempt to walk on the slippery rocks. Some are successful and some aren't!

For Information

Itasca State Park
Lake Itasca, MN 56460
(218) 266-3654

Location

Itasca State Park is located 20 miles north of Park Rapids on U.S. 71 in 3 counties: Clearwater, Hubbard, and Becker. At Itasca State Park, with an elevation 1,475 feet above sea level, the mighty Mississippi River begins its 2,552-mile journey to the Gulf of Mexico. Established in 1891 to preserve remnant stands of virgin pine and to protect the basin around the Mississippi's source, this 32,000-acre park has become a famous natural and cultural landmark in North America. It is the state's second largest park and the most developed park, yet also one of the most pristine. The most developed area is along the eastern arm of Lake Itasca.

Itasca State Park *(continued)*

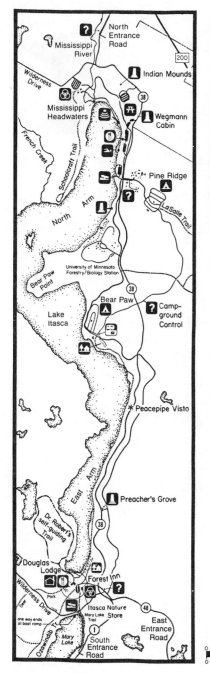

Just enjoying the view of Lake Itasca from a scenic overlook. Perhaps they can also catch a glimpse of the Chester Charles, *the only tour boat on beautiful Lake Itasca. The boat holds 50 passengers; all daily tours are narrated.*

Facilities & Activities

218 drive-in campsites at 2 campgrounds
5 backpack campsites
76 campsites with electricity
dump station
flush toilets (H)
vault toilets (H)
showers (H)
semi-modern group camp
rustic group camp
picnic area with open shelter
swimming
fishing (lake & stream)
boat launches
boat & canoe rentals
visitor center (seasonal)
interpretive program (year-round)
winter access
warming house
boat tours during summer
boat motor restrictions
lodge & cabins
snacks, food service, gift shop
motor rental
lookout tower
historic sites
bike rental
33 miles of foot trails
1.8 miles of self-guided trails
17 miles of bike trails
31 miles of X-country ski trails
31 miles of snowmobile trails

FACILITIES

- ? Information
- Picnic Area
- Interpretive Center
- Beach
- Boat Landing
- Historic Site
- Food Service
- Lodge
- Cabins
- Lookout Tower
- Campground
- Primitive Group Camp
- Walk-in Campsite
- Amphitheater
- Trailer Sanitation Station

TRAILS

- ········· Hiking
- —·—·— Interpretive
- ——— Bicycle/Hiking
- ✳ Point of Interest
- ✳ Overlook

Lake Bemidji State Park

For Information

Lake Bemidji State Park
3401 State Park Road N.E.
Bemidji, MN 56601
(218) 755-3843

Location

Lake Bemidji State Park is located on the northern shore of 6,765-acre lake Bemidji. Travel approximately 6 miles northeast of Bemidji via the old U.S. 71 highway, then 1.7 miles on County Road 21, then County Road 20 to the park entrance. The pine-moraine setting of this 1,688-acre park in Beltrami County affords visitors an enjoyable combination of Minnesota lake country recreation and the natural experiences of the northern forest. The name Bemidji came from Chief Bemidji, chief of the Chippewa tribe that lived around the lake.

Facilities & Activities

100 drive-in campsites
43 campsites with electricity
dump station
flush toilets (H)
vault toilets (H)
showers (H)
semi-modern group camp
rustic group camp
picnic area with enclosed shelter (H)
swimming
fishing (lake)
boat launch
boat rental
visitor center (year-round)
interpretive program (year-round)
winter access
warming house
14 miles of foot trails
1 mile of self-guided trails
1 mile of bike trails
10 miles of X-country ski trails
3 miles of snowmobile trails

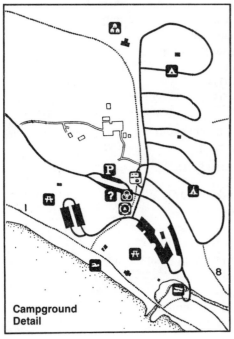

Campground Detail

FACILITIES

? Information	P Trail Parking	
☨ Picnic Area	⊙ Council Ring	
Beach	▲ Campground	
Boat Landing	Visitors Center (with modern winter trail center)	
Group Camp	Trailer Sanitation Station	
Primitive Group Camp		

TRAILS

.... Hiking
1.0 Trail Distances In Kilometers
* Scenic Overlook

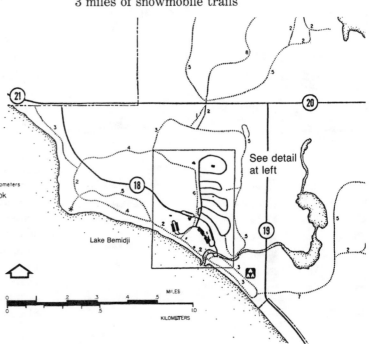

See detail at left

Lake Bemidji

MILES

KILOMETERS

Lake Bronson State Park

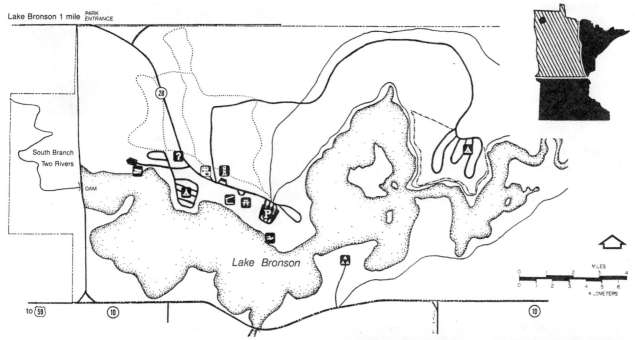

For Information

Lake Bronson State Park
Box 218
Lake Bronson, MN 56734
(218) 754-2200

Location

Lake Bronson State Park, in Kittson County, is located off of U.S. 59 and the city of Lake Bronson, 1 mile east on County Road 28. The 2,983-acre park is a fine example of the transition area between prairie to the west, and forest to the east. Lake Bronson, formed by damming the South Branch Two River, is a popular park for water related recreation as it is one of the few sizable bodies of water in the area.

No doubt these anglers are expecting fried fish fillets tonight and not hot dogs.

Facilities & Activities

190 drive-in campsites
2 canoe campsites
15 campsites with electricity
dump station
flush toilets (H)
vault toilets (H)
showers (H)
rustic group camp (50 capacity)
picnic area with open shelter
swimming

fishing (lake & river)
boat launch
boat & canoe rental
interpretive program (seasonal)
winter access
warming house
observation tower
snack bar
14 miles of foot trails
1 mile of self-guided trails
5 miles of bike trails
3 miles of X-country ski trails
10 miles of snowmobile trails

Lake Carlos State Park

For Information

Lake Carlos State Park
Rt. 2, Box 240
Carlos, MN 56319
(612) 852-7200

These sailors don't care whether Lake Carlos is 150 feet or 150 inches deep, as long as the wind blows.

Location

Lake Carlos State Park is located 10 miles north of Alexandria on State Highway 29 and 2 miles west on County Road 38 in Douglas County. The park's 1,250 acres lie within a hardwood transition zone between the prairies to the southwest and the coniferous forest to the northeast. Lake Carlos is a deep (150 feet deep in places), clean lake noted for its abundance of walleye, northern pike, bass and crappie. The outlet at the northeast corner is the source of the Long Prairie River.

Facilities & Activities

138 drive-in campsites in 2 campgrounds
46 campsites with electricity
dump station
flush toilets (H)
vault toilets (H)
showers (H)
horse camping
modern group camp (60 capacity)
rustic group camp
picnic area with open shelter (H)
swimming
fishing (lake)
boat launch on Lake Carlos
boat access (carry) on Hidden Lake
boat & canoe rental near park
visitor center (seasonal)
interpretive program (seasonal)
winter access
12.6 miles of foot trails
2.8 miles of self-guided trails
8 miles of horseback riding trails
5 miles of X-country ski trails
9 miles of snowmobile trails

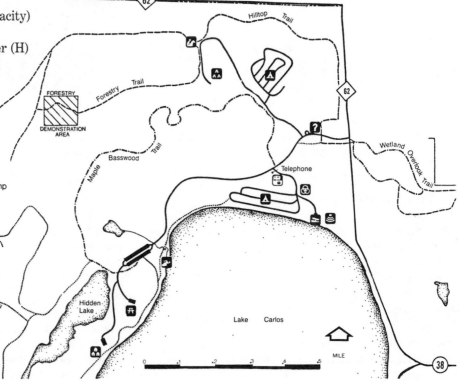

FACILITIES

- Group Camp
- ? Information
- Picnic Area
- Beach
- Boat Landing
- Amphitheater
- Primitive Group Camp
- Horseman's Area
- Trailer Sanitation Station
- Interpretive Center
- Campground

TRAILS

- —·—·— Interpretive
- ········· Hiking
- — — — Horseback/Hiking
- —·—·— Horseback/Interpretive

Lake Winnibigoshish Recreation Area

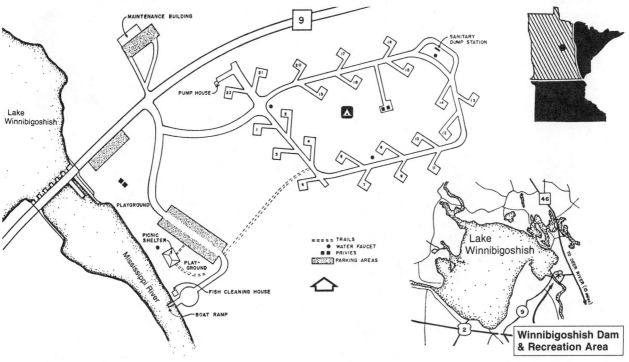

Statistics

67,000 acres in size
141 miles of shoreline
10-acre recreation area
operated & maintained by U.S. Army Corps of Engineers, St. Paul District

Resource Manager's Office

Lake Winnibigoshish Recreation Area
Inger Route
Deer River, MN 56636
(218) 246-8107

Facilities

22 camping sites
drinking water
restrooms
trailer dump station
picnic area/day use area
picnic shelter
playground
boat ramp
hiking trail
handicapped facilities
no reservations accepted

The boat ramp located at the recreation area below the dam provides convenient access to the Mississippi River below Lake Winnibigoshish.

Lake Winnibigoshish Dam was the first constructed in the system of six dams. It is located on the Mississippi River, 170 miles from its source in Lake Itasca.

Land O'Lakes State Forest
(Clint Converse Memorial Campground)

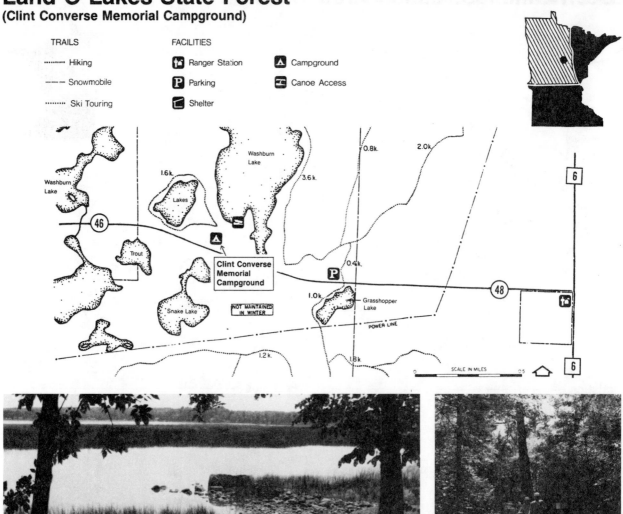

TRAILS

········· Hiking

— — — Snowmobile

········· Ski Touring

FACILITIES

Ranger Station

P Parking

Shelter

Campground

Canoe Access

Washburn Lake

1.6 k.

Lakes

Washburn Lake

46

Trout

Snake Lake

Clint Converse Memorial Campground

NOT MAINTAINED IN WINTER

0.8 k.

2.0 k.

3.6 k.

0.4 k.

1.0 k.

Grasshopper Lake

P

48

POWER LINE

1.2 k.

1.8 k.

SCALE IN MILES

6

6

Whether alone or with others, what a joy to hike the rock-strewn shoreline of a lake . . .

. . . or a forest trail lined with majestic trees. It's a sheer delight for body and mind!

For Information

Area Forest Supervisor
Box 34
Backus, MN 56435
(218) 947-3232

Location

From Outing, travel north on SH 6 for 2 miles to CR 48, turn left (west) and travel 2 miles.

Facilities

30 campsites
fee area
drinking water
7 picnic sites
swimming beach
water access
fishing
24-mile snowmobile trail
26-mile hiking & ski touring trail

Leech Lake Recreation Area

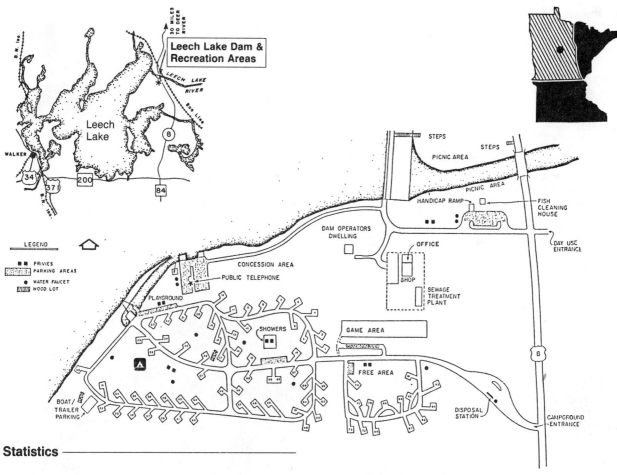

Leech Lake Dam & Recreation Areas

Statistics

126,000 acres in size
316 miles of shoreline
1,163 square-mile drainage area runoff (encompassing about 14 natural lakes) controlled by dam
75-acre recreation area
operated & maintained by U.S. Army Corps of Engineers, St. Paul District

playground
game area
boat ramp
handicapped facilities
no reservations accepted

Resource Manager's Office

Leech Lake Recreation Area
Federal Dam, MN 56641
(218) 654-3145

Facilities

74 camping sites
60 sites with electricity
drinking water
showers
restrooms
trailer dump station
picnic area/day use area

Wild rice is abundant along the shoreline of Leech Lake and is harvested yearly.

Maplewood State Park

For Information

Maplewood State Park
Rt. 3, Box 422
Pelican Rapids, MN 56572
(218) 863-8383

Location

Maplewood State Park is located 7 miles east of Pelican Rapids, on State Highway 108 in Ottertail County. On a series of high hills, the park provides a respite from the intensively farmed lands that surround it. The highest hills in the park approach 1,600 feet. The tree-covered hills provide striking vistas of small, clear lakes nestled in deep valleys. The many attractions of this 9,250-acre park offer people a variety of recreational opportunities throughout the year.

Facilities & Activities

61 drive-in campsites at 3 locations
3 backpack campsites
2 canoe campsites
flush toilets (H)
vault toilets
showers (H)

horse camping
rustic group camp
picnic area
group picnic area
swimming
fishing (lake)
2 boat launches
boat access (carry)
boat & canoe rental
winter access
Wilson Lake Cabin (modern A-frame house; beds for 14 people)
25 miles of foot trails
1 mile of self-guided trail
15 miles of horseback riding trails
17 miles of X-country ski trails
14 miles of snowmobile trails

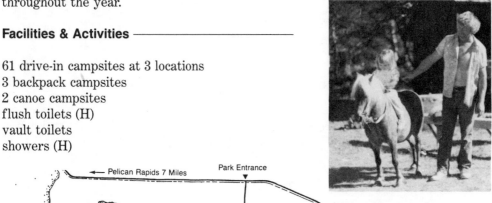

This horse camping family even brought the pony for the young 'un. There are 15 miles of riding trails available at Maplewood State Park. I wonder how many miles this horse and rider made?

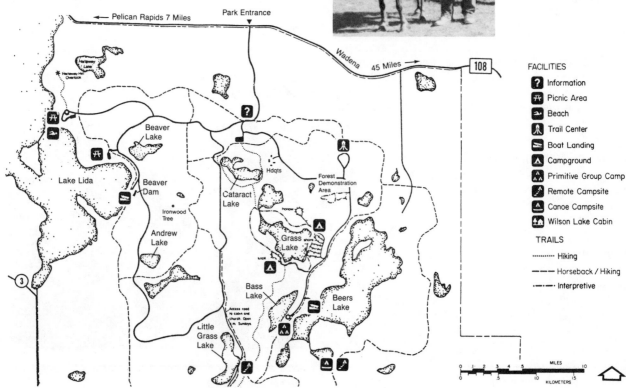

Mille Lacs Kathio State Park

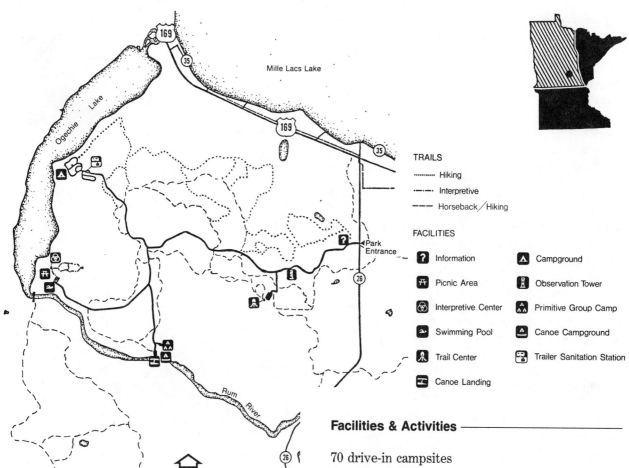

Mille Lacs Lake

Ogechie Lake

Rum River

TRAILS
- .... Hiking
- --·--· Interpretive
- — — Horseback / Hiking

FACILITIES

?	Information	▲	Campground
🎪	Picnic Area	🔭	Observation Tower
☯	Interpretive Center	⛺	Primitive Group Camp
🏊	Swimming Pool	⛺	Canoe Campground
🚶	Trail Center	🚐	Trailer Sanitation Station
🛶	Canoe Landing		

MILES

KILOMETERS

For Information

Mille Lacs Kathio State Park
HC 67, Box 85
Onamia, MN 56359
(612) 532-3523

Location

Mille Lacs Kathio State Park is located 8 miles northwest of Onamia on U.S. 169 in Mille Lacs County. Take County Road 26 1 mile to the park entrance. Mille Lacs Kathio, over 10,000 acres in size, is the fourth largest state park in Minnesota. Mille Lacs Lake is the source of the Rum River, which flows through the park and eventually joins the Mississippi River 146 miles downstream at Anoka. Lake Ogechie, the long shallow lake near the campground, has historically been noted for its lush growth of wild rice.

Facilities & Activities

70 drive-in campsites
4 canoe campsites
dump station
flush toilets (H)
vault toilets
showers (H)
horse camping
rustic group camp (50 capacity)
picnic area (H)
swimming pond
fishing (lake & river)
3 boat launches
boat & canoe rentals
interpretive center/museum (seasonal)
interpretive program (seasonal)
winter access
warming house
ski rentals
100-foot observation tower
historic site
35 miles of foot trails
2 miles of self-guided trails
27 horseback riding trails
18 miles of X-country ski trails
19 miles of snowmobile trails

Old Mill State Park

For Information

Old Mill State Park
Rt. 1, Box 42
Argyle, MN 56713
(218) 437-8174

Location

Old Mill State Park is located in Marshall County, approximately half-way between Argyle (on U.S. 75) and Newfolden (on U.S. 59) off of County Road 4. The park entrance is ½ mile north on County Road 39. Old Mill State Park is like an undisturbed island in a sea of crop land. It contains examples of the landscape as first seen by the settlers over a century ago. The old grist mill is the focal point of this 237-acre park. On one or more days each summer, the mill is operated for visitors. This gives a feeling of the history of the Red River Valley. A restored cabin can be found near the mill adding to this feeling.

Facilities & Activities

26 drive-in campsites
10 campsites with electricity
flush toilets (H)
vault toilets (H)
showers (H)
rustic group camp
picnic area with enclosed shelter (H)
swimming pond
fishing (stream)
interpretive program (seasonal)
winter access
warming house
skating rink
old grist mill
historic site
7 miles of foot trails
1 mile of self-guided trail
3 miles of X-country ski trails
3 miles of snowmobile trails

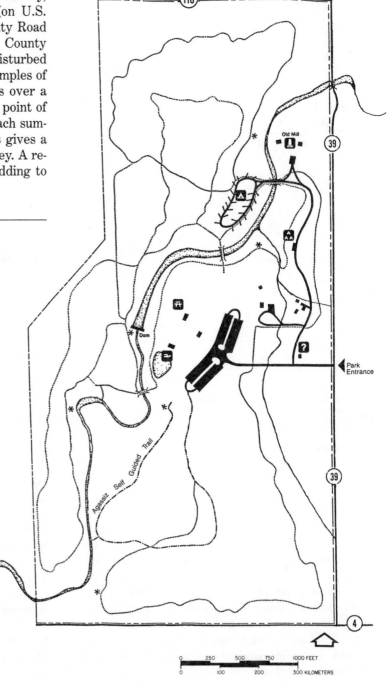

TRAILS

·········· Hiking

—··— Interpretive

∗ Overlook

FACILITIES

Information
Picnic Area
Beach
Campground
Primitive Group Camp
Historic Site

Paul Bunyan State Forest

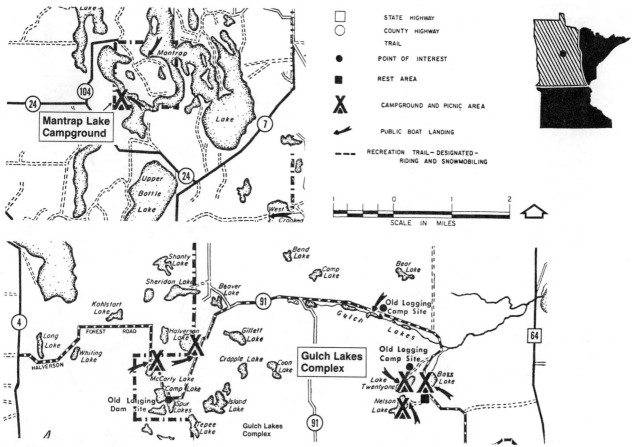

STATE HIGHWAY
COUNTY HIGHWAY
TRAIL
POINT OF INTEREST
REST AREA
CAMPGROUND AND PICNIC AREA
PUBLIC BOAT LANDING
RECREATION TRAIL – DESIGNATED –
RIDING AND SNOWMOBILING

SCALE IN MILES

For Information

Area Forest Supervisor
Box 113, 607 W. 1st St.
Park Rapids, MN 56470
(218) 732-3309

Mantrap Lake Campground

Location

From Park Rapids, travel 12 miles north on CR 4,
1½ miles east on CR 24, ¾ mile north on CR 104.

Facilities

38 campsites
fee area
drinking water
5 picnic sites
swimming
water access
fishing
2-mile nature & ski-touring trail

Gulch Lakes Recreation Area

For Information

Area Forest Supervisor
2220 Bemidji Avenue
Bemidji, MN 56601
(218) 755-2890

Location

The Gulch Lakes complex can be reached via the
Halverson Forest Road east from CR 4 (south of
Lake George) and on the Gulch Lake Forest Road
west from SH 64.

Facilities

12 campsites at 5 individual units   water access
11 picnic sites   fishing
swimming   hiking trails

Pillsbury State Forest

(Rock Lake Campground)

For Information

Area Forest Supervisor
1601 Minnesota Drive
Brainerd, MN 56401
(218) 828-2565

Facilities

18 campsites
fee area
drinking water
4 picnic sites
swimming
water access
fishing
8-mile hiking/ski-touring trail

Location

From Pillager, take SH 210 west for ½ mile to CR 1, turn right (north) and travel 7 miles, turn left (west) on the forest road and follow signs.

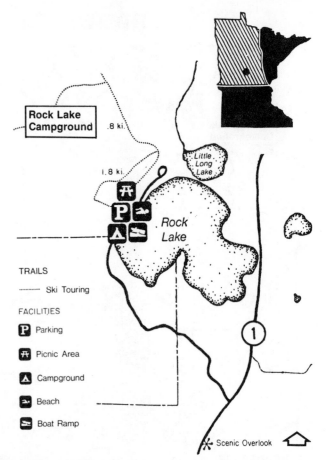

A striking snow scene! Is it the first snow of the season or is Spring just around the corner?

There's enough outdoor excitement in Minnesota to make anybody as "crazy as a loon," which is the state bird. (See pages 1–24 for what the North Star State has to offer.)

Minnesota Dept. of Natural Resources

Minnesota Dept. of Natural Resources

Minnesota Dept. of Natural Resources

Known as "the land of 10,000 lakes," Minnesota actually has about 12,000 lakes that are 10 acres or larger.

Contrary to some native's opinions, Minnesota has 4 distinct seasons, with autumn being amply heralded by spectacular displays (page 2).

N.L. Gilchrest

Camping along the shore of Lake Superior is like camping by an ocean. (See page 64 for parks along the lake.)

*Minnesota is a canoeing
paradise, but remember that
some portages are easier . . .*

. . . than others (page 19).

*Among other things, camping
teaches patience, and that's
just what you'll need to see
the flat-tailed occupant of
this residence.*

*It's obvious why Camden
State Park was considered
an oasis by early pioneers
(page 109).*

Canoe her cold blue, glacier-gouged lakes, and you"ll clearly understand why the Sioux Indians called this territory "Minnesota," which means "sky tinted water."

Banning State Park's spectacular rapids provide some of the state's most challenging canoeing and kayaking adventures (page 65).

For more leisurely water sports and excellent bird watching, Lake Shetek State Park is "just what the camper ordered" (page 123).

Minnesota has its share of thrashin', splashin' white-water, white-knuckle fun (page 20)!

But names can be misleading—Whitewater State Park (page 136) is named after a lazy river running through it that sometimes turns milky white when heavy spring rains wash clay deposits into it.

When you're hiking in Minnesota's splendid outdoors, don't forget to look up—or you might miss a magnificent bald eagle! Chippewa National Forest (page 31) is home to the largest breeding population of bald eagles in the lower 48 states.

Split Rock Lighthouse State Park offers a terrific panorama of Lake Superior . . .

. . . and is Minnesota's first "cart-in" campground (page 89).

Even when you're just heading out for a day hike (page 13), keep your camera handy . . .

. . . because some of the locals . . .

. . . might be out hiking, too!

High Falls in Tettegouche State Park (page 101) is but one of the several waterfalls and cascades you'll find throughout the North Star State. (See page 2 for a list.)

M. Little

M. Little

Itasca State Park is one of Minnesota's most pristine parks . . .

. . . and it offers campers the unique opportunity of walking across the mighty Mississippi River (page 44).

Minnesota Dept. of Natural Resources

M. Little

Most of the state's parks offer great fishing, and there's a lot more elbow room than these young anglers would have you believe.

The variety of Minnesota's great outdoors is nowhere more evident than in Zippel Bay State Park, which has 15 miles of snowmobile trails for winter campers (page 18), and 3 miles of some of the state's finest sand beach for summer campers (page 62).

Minnesota's parks and forests offer many miles of bicycle trails (page 15), so if you don't want to hike, bring a bike!

Jay Cooke State Park offers campers a unique blend of rugged rock formations and beautiful hardwood forests (page 76).

With all the waterfalls and cascades in Minnesota (page 2), it's a safe bet that a few of the state's 25,000 + miles of rivers and streams are vertical!

Covering more than 1 million acres, the Boundary Waters Canoe Area is the nation's only designated canoe wilderness (pages 2 and 23).

These pelicans are just a sample of the waterfowl you'll see at Monson Lake State Park, one of the state's top birding spots (page 126).

The North Star State has more than 1,800 miles of cross-country ski trails, and if you're between ages 16–64, you'll probably need a pass to ski them (page 18).

The fun and adventure you'll find in Minnesota's wonderful outdoors is as good as gold!

Fishing is a year-round sport in Minnesota, especially on Lake Mille Lacs, which is known as the ice fishing capital of the world (page 53).

Pokegama Lake Recreation Area

Statistics

16,000 acres in size
53 miles of shoreline
10-acre recreation area
operated & maintained by U.S. Army Corps of Engineers, St. Paul District

Resource Manager's Office

Pokegama Lake Recreation Area
3810 West Hwy. 2
Grand Rapids, MN 55744
(218) 326-6128

Facilities

16 camping sites
4 sites with electricity
drinking water
rest rooms
trailer dump station
picnic area/day use area
picnic shelter
playground
boat ramp
interpretive trail
handicapped facilities
no reservations accepted

This recreation area is popular for at least two reasons: its location along U.S. Highway 2 makes it a convenient stopover point for vacationers traveling east-west; and, the area below the dam is said to be a very popular fishing spot for "lunkers."

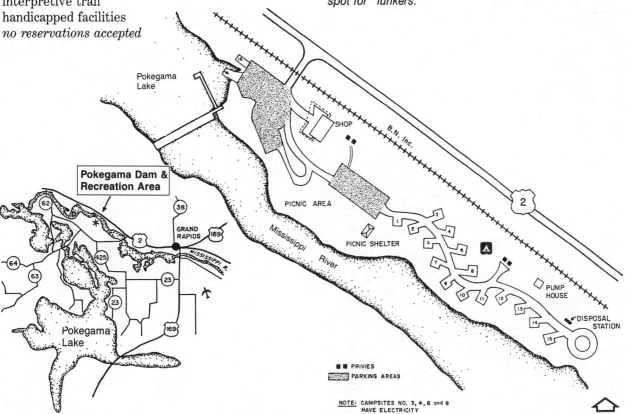

Ronald Louis Cloutier Recreation Area

Statistics

13,600 acres in size (Pine River Reservoir, also
known as Whitefish Chain of Lakes)
119 miles of shoreline
562 square-mile drainage area runoff (encompassing 15 natural lakes) controlled by dam
42-acre recreation area
operated & maintained by U.S. Army Corps of Engineers, St. Paul District

Resource Manager's Office

Ronald Louis Cloutier Recreation Area
Box 36
Cross Lake, MN 56442
(218) 692-4488

Facilities

117 camping sites
38 sites with electricity
drinking water
showers
restrooms
trailer dump station
picnic area/day use area
playground
games area
swimming area
boat ramp
canoe launch
handicapped facilities
no reservations accepted

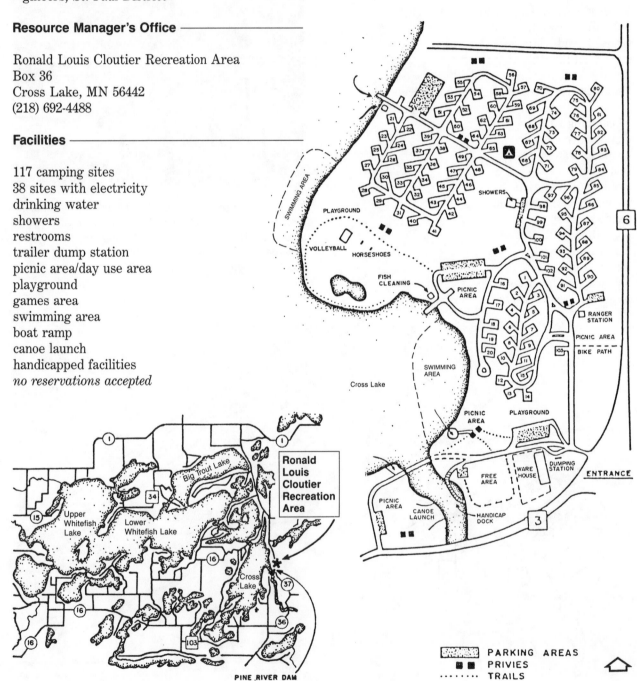

Schoolcraft State Park

For Information

Schoolcraft State Park
HCR 4, Box 181
Deer River, MN 56636
(218) 566-2383

Location

Schoolcraft State Park, located on the Mississippi River in Cass County, contains 295 acres, much of which is virgin pine timber. The park may be reached by traveling west from Deer River on U.S. 2, then south on County Road 3, then County Road 74 to the park entrance. Another approach to the park is to travel southeast from Deer River on U.S. 2, then south on State Highway 6, west on County Road 65, and north on County Road 74 to the park entrance. The park was named for Henry Rowe Schoolcraft, discoverer of the headwaters of the "Mighty Mississippi," and a long time agent for the Chippewa Indians at Sault Saint Marie. The rustic campground is closed during the winter months.

Facilities & Activities

38 drive-in rustic campsites
12 canoe campsites
vault toilets
rustic group camp
picnic area
fishing (river)
boat launch
2 miles of foot trails
1 mile of self-guided trail

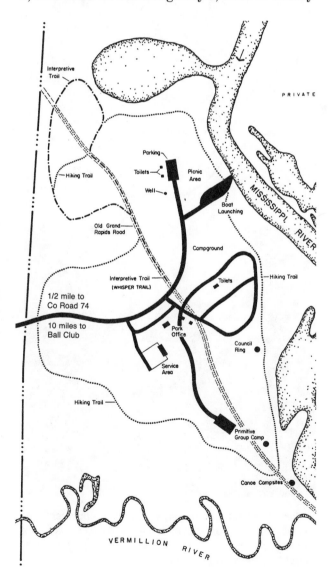

These inquisitive nature lovers could easily fall into the Mississippi River if they're not careful. Wonder what's so intriguing?

Terry R. Johnson Recreation Area

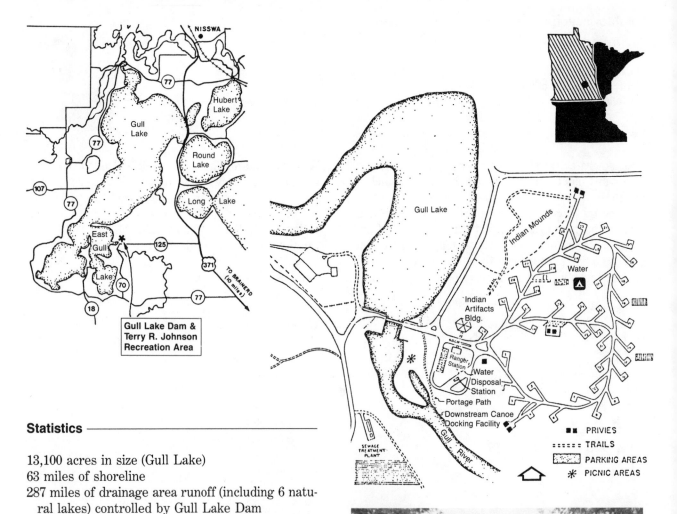

Statistics

13,100 acres in size (Gull Lake)

63 miles of shoreline

287 miles of drainage area runoff (including 6 natural lakes) controlled by Gull Lake Dam

82-acre recreation area

operated & maintained by U.S. Army Corps of Engineers, St. Paul District

Resource Manager's Office

Terry R. Johnson Recreation Area
Rt. 10
Brainerd, MN 56401
(218) 829-3334

Facilities

39 camping sites
10 sites with electricity
drinking water
showers
restrooms
trailer dump station
picnic area/day use area
playground

swimming beach
change house
boat ramp
canoe launch
interpretive trail/display
handicapped facilities
no reservations accepted

Indian artifacts are displayed in the interpretive center at the Terry R. Johnson Recreation Area. A trail leads to the Indian burial mounds. The mounds are listed on the National Register of Historic Places.

Two Inlets State Forest
(Hungryman Lake Campground)

For Information

Area Forest Supervisor
607 West 1st St., Box 113
Park Rapids, MN 56470
(218) 732-3309

Location

From the village of Two Inlets, travel 2 miles east on CR 46, then north for 1 mile. Access from the east is via SH 71 and CR 41.

Facilities

14 campsites	fishing
fee area	hiking trail
drinking water	27.5 miles of snowmobile trails
3 picnic sites	
swimming	
water access	

"Oops, the water's cold! Maybe I'll just walk on it, instead."

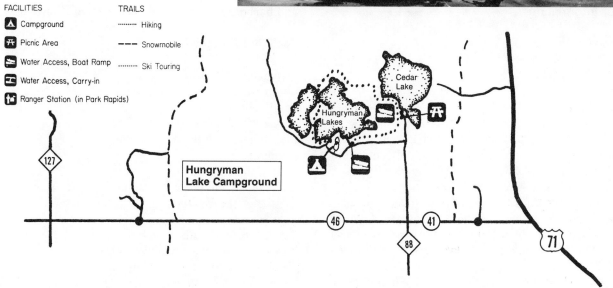

FACILITIES

⛺ Campground
🛆 Picnic Area
Water Access, Boat Ramp
Water Access, Carry-in
Ranger Station (in Park Rapids)

TRAILS

.... Hiking
– – – Snowmobile
.... Ski Touring

Cedar Lake

Hungryman Lakes

Hungryman Lake Campground

127

46

88

41

71

Zippel Bay State Park

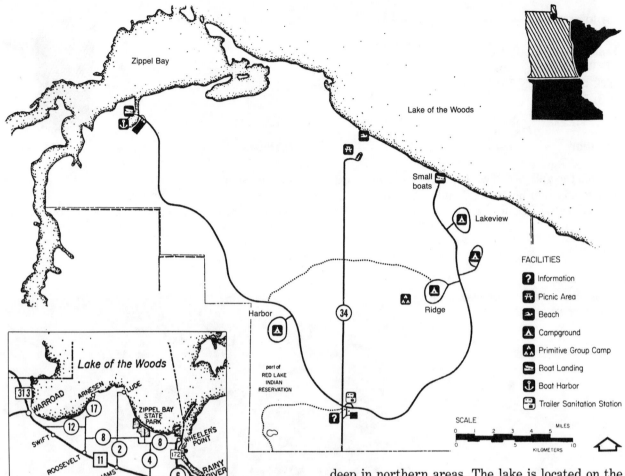

For Information

Zippel Bay State Park
Williams, MN 56686
(218) 783-6252

Location

Zippel Bay State Park is located 10 miles northeast of Williams on County Road 8, between State Highway 172 and County Road 2 (see vicinity map). Located on Beautiful Lake of the Woods, the 2,946-acre park includes 3 miles of what many consider the finest sand beach in the entire state. Lake of the Woods is ocean-like in its size and moods. It has 65,000 miles of shoreline, 14,000 islands, is 55 miles wide at its widest and varies in depth from 4 to 35 feet deep in the southern bays to more than 150 feet deep in northern areas. The lake is located on the border between Minnesota and Canada and possesses historical interest of national significance; this great border lake is where the Voyageurs journeyed by water as early as 1700. The boat launch and harbor are in the sheltered calm of Zippel Bay.

Facilities & Activities

60 drive-in campsites
dump station
vault toilets (H)
rustic group camp
picnic area with open shelter (H)
swimming
fishing (lake/stream)
boat launch and docks on Zippel Bay with access to
   Lake of the Woods
winter access
6 miles of foot trails
6 miles of horseback riding trails
2 miles of X-country ski trails
15 miles of snowmobile trails

Other State Forest Campgrounds in Region I

State Forest Campgrounds	No. of Campsites	Camping Fee	Drinking Water	No. of Picnic Sites	Swimming	Water Access	Fishing
Big Fork State Forest Long Lake	12		X	2		X	X
Birch Lakes State Forest Birch Lake	29	X	X	8	X	X	X
Bowstring State Forest Cottonwood Lake	15		X	1	X	X	X
Forestry Administered Facilities Moose Lake	12	X	X			X	X
Red Lake State Forest Waskish	33	X	X	10	X	X	X
White Earth State Forest Arrow Point	6				X		X

(See page 27 for locations)

The Minnesota Office of Tourism offers a 50-page booklet on the state's 11,000 + miles of marked, groomed snowmobile trails (page 18).

Arrow Point Campground
Area Forest Supervisor
2220 Bemidji Avenue
Bemidji, MN 56601
(218) 755-2890

Campground maps and/or maps of the state forest area where the campground is located are unavailable for 6 of the state forest campgrounds in Region 1. Therefore, the information presented here is a somewhat different format than the information on the campgrounds located in the other 19 state forests.

For Information

Long Lake, Cottonwood, & Moose Lake
 Campgrounds
Area Forest Supervisor
Box 157
Deer River, MN 56636
(218) 246-8343

Birch Lake Campground
Area Forest Supervisor
915 South Highway #65
Cambridge, MN 55008
(612) 689-2832

Waskish Campground
Area Forest Supervisor
Blackduck, MN 56630
(218) 835-6684

Location

Long Lake Campground—From Talmoon, take SH 6 north for 6 miles.

Birch Lake Campground—From Melrose, take CR 13 north for 5.5 miles to CR 17; turn right (east) and travel 1.5 miles; turn left (north) and go 2 miles; then turn right (east) on forest road.

Cottonwood Lake Campground—From Deer River, take SH 6 north for 4 miles to CR 19; turn right (east) and go 3 miles; turn left (north) on CR 48 and travel 1 mile; then turn right (east) and follow signs about 1 mile.

Moose Lake Campground—From Deer River, take SH 6 north for 4 miles to CR 19; turn right (east) and go 5.5 miles; turn left (north) on CR 238 for 1 mile.

Waskish Campground—On SH 72 at Waskish just south of bridge.

Arrow Point Campground—From Park Rapids, go 17 miles north on U.S. 71; then 19 miles west on SH 113; then north for 5 miles on Height of Land forest road; walk east for .5 mile.

Region 2

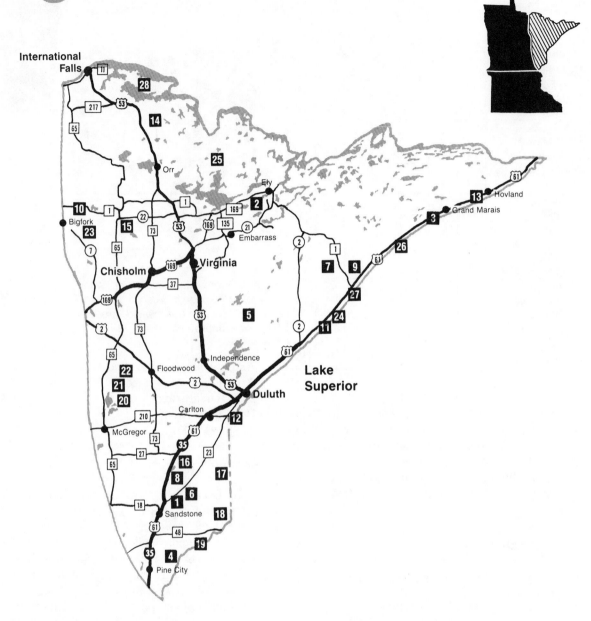

International Falls
11
28
217
53
14
65
25
Orr
1
10
1
22
15
73
53
Bigfork
23
65
7
Chisholm
169
37
169
2
73
53
22
Floodwood
21
2
53
20
Carlton
210
61
McGregor
73
35
27
16
65
8
18
1
Sandstone
61
35
48
4
Pine City

Ely
169
2
135
21
Embarrass
Virginia
5

61
13 Hovland
3 Grand Marais
26
2
1
7
9
27
24
11

Lake Superior
Independence
Duluth
12
23
17
6
18
19

1—Banning State Park, 65	15—McCarthy Beach State Park, 79
2—Bear Head Lake State Park, 66	16—Moose Lake Recreation Area, 80
3—Cascade River State Park, 67	17—Nemadji State Forest, 81
4—Chengwatana State Forest, 68	18—St. Croix State Forest, 82
5—Cloquet Valley State Forest, 69	19—St. Croix State Park, 83–84
6—D. A. R. Memorial State Forest, 69	20—Sandy Lake Recreation Area, 85
7—Finland State Forest, 70	21—Savanna Portage State Park, 86
8—General C. C. Andrews State Forest, 71	22—Savanna State Forest, 87
9—George H. Crosby-Manitou State Park, 72	23—Scenic State Park, 88
10—George Washington State Forest, 73–74	24—Split Rock Lighthouse State Park, 89
11—Gooseberry Falls State Park, 75	25—Superior National Forest, 90–99
12—Jay Cooke State Park, 76	26—Temperance River State Park, 100
13—Judge C. R. Magney State Park, 77	27—Tettegouche State Park, 101
14—Kabetogama State Forest, 78	28—Voyageurs National Park, 102–103

Banning State Park

For Information

Banning State Park
P.O. Box V
Sandstone, MN 55072
(612) 245-2668

Location

Banning State Park is located in Pine County, 4 miles north of the city of Sandstone. The park entrance is off I-35 and State Highway 23. The 6,237-acre park constitutes land adjacent to a 10-mile stretch of the Kettle River valley, a state wild and scenic river. The Banning Rapids, a high scenic portion of the Kettle River, comprises 5 spectacular segments: Blueberry Slide, Mother's Delight, Dragon's Tooth, Little Banning, and, finally, Hell's Gate. These rapids provide one of the state's most challenging river experiences for canoeing and kayaking.

Campers at state parks should stop at the entry station to register and pay fees prior to driving to the campground.

Facilities & Activities

31 drive-in campsites
4 canoe campsites
flush toilets (H)
vault toilets (H)
picnic area (H)
fishing (river)
boat launches
visitor center (seasonal)
winter access
historic site—Banning Townsite and Sandstone
   Quarry
14 miles of foot trails
1.8 miles of self-guided trails
11 miles of X-country ski trails
5 miles of snowmobile trails

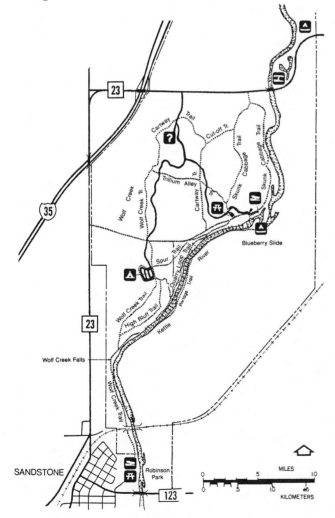

FACILITIES		TRAILS
? Information	**≥** Water Access - Boat Ramp	•••••• Hiking
⛽ Picnic Area	**⇄** Water Access - Carry-in	1.5 TRAIL MILEAGE
▲ Campground	**▲** Canoe Campsite	* Overlook

Bear Head Lake State Park

For Information

Bear Head Lake State Park
Star Route 2, Box 5700
Ely, MN 55731
(218) 365-4253

Location

Bear Head Lake State Park is located 18 miles east of Tower in St. Louis County. Travel State Highway 1/169 east toward Ely to County Road 128, then south on 128 for 6 miles to the park. Bear Head Lake State Park's 4,375 acres surround Bear Head Lake. The park also holds 3 other fishing lakes. The northern forest that surrounds the 674-acre Bear Head Lake is home to a variety of wild life. Fishing, boating, and the beautiful sand swimming beach are visitor favorites at this remote northern park.

A summer stroll along the banks of the North Bay of Bear Head Lake in early morning or late afternoon could reward you with a sighting, or at least a hearing, of the common loon.

Facilities & Activities

73 drive-in campsites
5 backpack campsites
2 canoe campsites
dump station
flush toilets (H)
vault toilets (H)
showers (H)
rustic group camp
picnic area (H)
swimming
fishing (stream & lake)
boat launch
boat & canoe rental
winter access
17 miles of foot trails
14 miles of X-country ski trails
6 miles of snowmobile trails that link with the Taconite Trail

FACILITIES

🛈 Information
🏕 Picnic Area
🏊 Beach
🚢 Boat Landing

🏕 Campground
🏕 Primitive Group Camp
🎒 Backpack Camping
🏕 Water Accessible Camping

TRAILS

········· Hiking
‒ ‒ ‒ Horseback/Hiking

Cascade River State Park

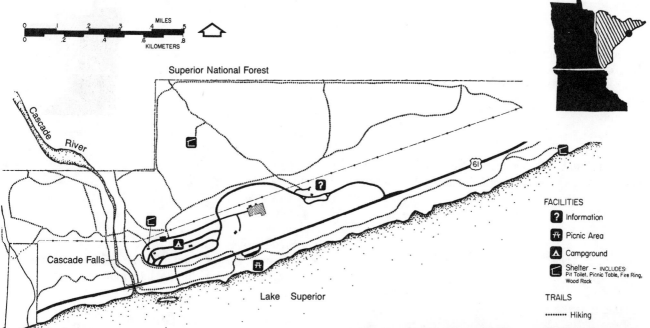

FACILITIES

? Information

🏕 Picnic Area

▲ Campground

Shelter – INCLUDES:
Pit Toilet, Picnic Table, Fire Ring, Wood Rack

TRAILS

•••••••• Hiking

Beautiful waterfalls may be viewed from trails along either side of the Cascade River. Motorists traveling U.S. Highway 61 should definitely plan to stop long enough to see Cascade Falls.

For Information

Cascade River State Park
HCR 3, Box 450
Lutsen, MN 55612
(218) 387-1543

Location

Cascade River State Park is located in Cook County on US 61, 21 miles northeast of Tofte and 9 miles southwest of Grand Marais. This 2,813-acre park along Lake Superior, contains a diversity of settings; the beautiful Cascade River; Indian Camp, Spruce, and Cutface creeks; and the rugged Lake Superior shoreline. Park trails lead from Lake Superior up to the height of the Sawtooth Mountains and their panoramic view of the North Shore.

Facilities & Activities

37 drive-in campsites
5 backpack campsites
dump station near park
flush toilets (H)
vault toilets (H)
showers (H)
rustic group camp

picnic area with enclosed shelter (H)
fishing (lake & river)
winter access
warming house
15 miles of foot trails
30 miles of X-country ski trails
4 miles of snowmobile trails

REGION 2

Chengwatana State Forest
(Snake River Campground)

For Information

Area Forest Supervisor
Route 2, 701 South Kenwood
Moose Lake, MN 55767
(218) 485-4474

Location

From Pine City, travel CR 8 east for 6 miles, continue east on CR 118 for 3 miles to the entrance road.

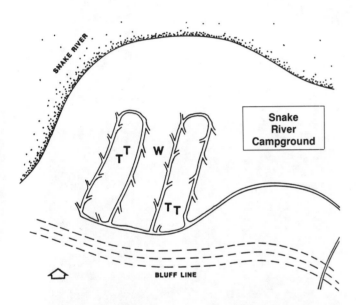

Facilities

26 campsites
fee area
drinking water
8 picnic sites
fishing
On Snake River canoe route
½-mile from access point for an 8-mile ski touring/ hiking trail and a 20-mile snowmobile trail

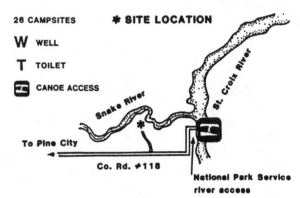

Old Man Winter does a masterful job of decorating the Minnesota landscape with snow.

Cloquet Valley State Forest
(Indian Lake Campground)

FACILITIES

Water Access (trailer)

Campground

For Information

Area Forest Supervisor
6163 Rice Lake Road
Duluth, MN 55803
(218) 723-4669

Location

On Cloquet River; from Rollins, travel 1 mile north on CR 44.

Facilities

8 campsites
fee area
drinking water
4 picnic sites
swimming
water access
fishing

D.A.R.* Memorial State Forest
(D.A.R. Campground)

For Information

Area Forest Supervisor
Route 2, 701 South Denwood
Moose Lake, MN 55767
(218) 485-4474

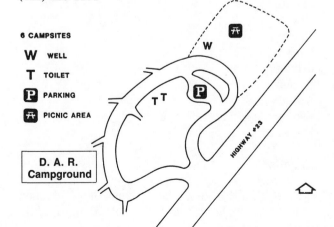

6 CAMPSITES

W   WELL

T   TOILET

P   PARKING

🛆   PICNIC AREA

D. A. R. Campground

Location

From Askov, take SH 23 northeast for 2 miles.

Facilities

6 campsites
fee area
drinking water
2 picnic sites
*Daughters of the American Revolution

Finland State Forest

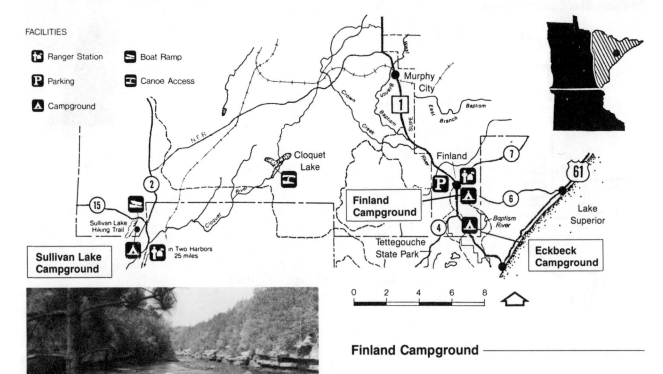

FACILITIES

- 🏠 Ranger Station
- 🅿 Parking
- ⛺ Campground
- 🚤 Boat Ramp
- 🛶 Canoe Access

Finland Campground

Sullivan Lake Campground

Eckbeck Campground

The Banning Rapids, a high scenic portion of the Kettle River, provide one of the state's most challenging river experiences for canoeing and kayaking.

For Information (for all 3 campgrounds)

Area Forest Supervisor
6163 Rice Lake Road
Duluth, MN 55803
(218) 723-4669

Eckbeck Campground

Facilities

31 campsites
fee area
drinking water
4 picnic sites
fishing

Location

Located on the Baptism River near the North Shore, 3 miles south of Finland on SH 1.

Finland Campground

Facilities

21 campsites
fee area
drinking water
10 picnic sites
fishing

Location

Located on the Baptism River. From Finland, travel ½ mile east on CR 6.

Sullivan Lake Campground

Facilities

10 campsites
fee area
drinking water
2 picnic sites
water access
fishing (designated trout lake)
hiking trail

Location

From Two Harbors, take CR 2 north for 26 miles to CR 15, turn left (west) for ½ mile, then turn left (south) for ½ mile.

General C. C. Andrews State Forest

(Willow River Campground)

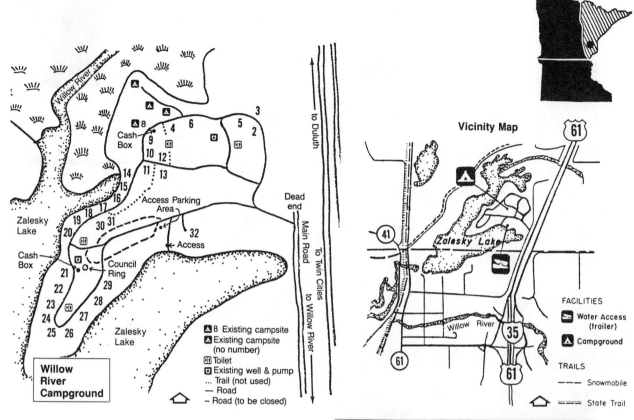

Willow River Campground

Cash Box

Cash Box

Zalesky Lake

Council Ring

Access Parking Area

Access

Dead end

to Duluth

Main Road

To Twin Cities

to Willow River

Zalesky Lake

🔺8 Existing campsite
🔺 Existing campsite (no number)
🚻 Toilet
🚰 Existing well & pump
... Trail (not used)
— Road
- Road (to be closed)

Vicinity Map

FACILITIES

🏊 Water Access (trailer)
🏕 Campground

TRAILS

– – – Snowmobile
═══ State Trail

Zalesky Lake

Willow River

For Information

Area Forest Supervisor
Route 2, 701 South Kenwood
Moose Lake, MN 55767
(218) 485-4474

Location

From the village of Willow River, travel east on North St. to service road of IH-35, turn left (north) and travel ½ mile.

Facilities

41 campsites
fee area
drinking water
water access
fishing
group camping

Is this a bird-watching cyclist? . . . or is she trying to locate the rest of her cycling group?

George H. Crosby—Manitou State Park

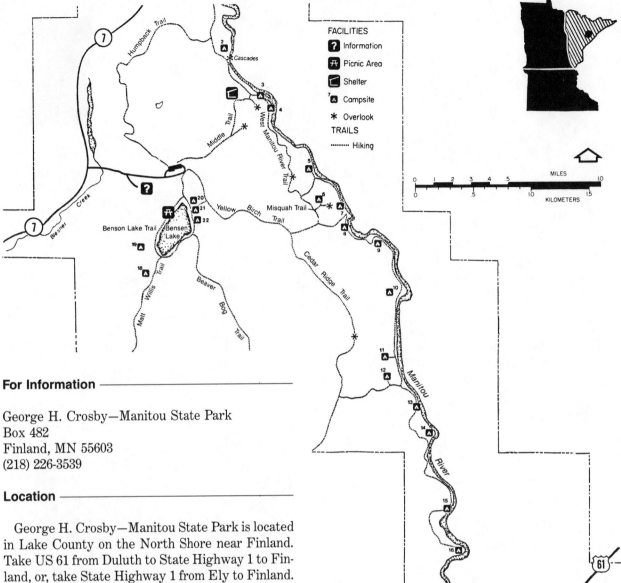

FACILITIES

? Information

⛤ Picnic Area

◢ Shelter

⑦⬛ Campsite

✳ Overlook

TRAILS

········· Hiking

MILES

KILOMETERS

For Information

George H. Crosby—Manitou State Park
Box 482
Finland, MN 55603
(218) 226-3539

Location

George H. Crosby—Manitou State Park is located in Lake County on the North Shore near Finland. Take US 61 from Duluth to State Highway 1 to Finland, or, take State Highway 1 from Ely to Finland. At Finland, take County Road 7 the 8 miles to the park entrance. The Manitou River cascades through a rugged river valley to Lake Superior. Along this gorge, visitors to this 3,400-acre park can enjoy the river's wild beauty.

About the Park

The park offers the opportunity of camping in isolated backpack sites along the Manitou River. Rugged park trails that will test your hiking abilities lead backpackers into the depths of the park, into the habitat of black bears and timber wolves. All campsites are off the trail, are designated, have primitive toilets, but no drinking water. Winter camping is possible. All trails can be snowshoed and

some are for advanced X-country skiers. Snow usually remains on the ground from November through April.

Facilities & Activities

21 backpack campsites
vault toilets (H)
walk-in picnic area (H)
fishing (stream & lake)
boat access (carry)
winter access
23 miles of foot trails
11 miles of X-country ski trails

George Washington State Forest

About the Forest

This state forest was created by the state legislature in 1931 to commemorate the 200th anniversary of the birth of our first president. Within its boundaries are 200 lakes totaling over 15,000 acres. There are 6 primitive campgrounds, 20 miles of hiking/ski-touring trails, and over 200 miles of groomed scenic trails for the snowmobilers.

For Information

(for Bear Lake, Button Box Lake, & Thistledew Lake Campgrounds)

Area Forest Supervisor
Box 705
Hibbing, MN 55746
(218) 262-6760

(for Larson Lake, Lost Lake, & Owen Lake Campgrounds)

Area Forest Supervisor
Box 157
Deer River, MN 56636
(218) 246-8343

Locations

Bear Lake Campground—from Nashwauk, travel north for 23 miles on SH 65 to CR 52 (Venning Road); turn left (west) and go 2 miles; then turn left (south) for 2.5 miles.

Button Box Lake Campground—from Togo, take SH 1 west for 4.5 miles, then northwest for 4 miles.

Larson Lake Campground—from Effie, take SH 1 east for 11 miles to Bass Lake Road; turn right (south), travel 2 miles to junction; then turn right (west) and go 1 mile.

Lost Lake and Owen Lake Campgrounds—from Bigfork, take CR 7 (Scenic Highway) southeast for 10 miles to CR 340; turn left (east) and go about 7 miles to ranger station; turn left (north) across from ranger station and follow signs for 2 miles.

Thistledew Lake Campground—from Togo, go 4.5 miles west on SH 1, then 2 miles south (left).

. . . a beautiful place to be . . . whether you're fishing or whether you're just watching!

There's at least 3 people in this family who like to paddle.

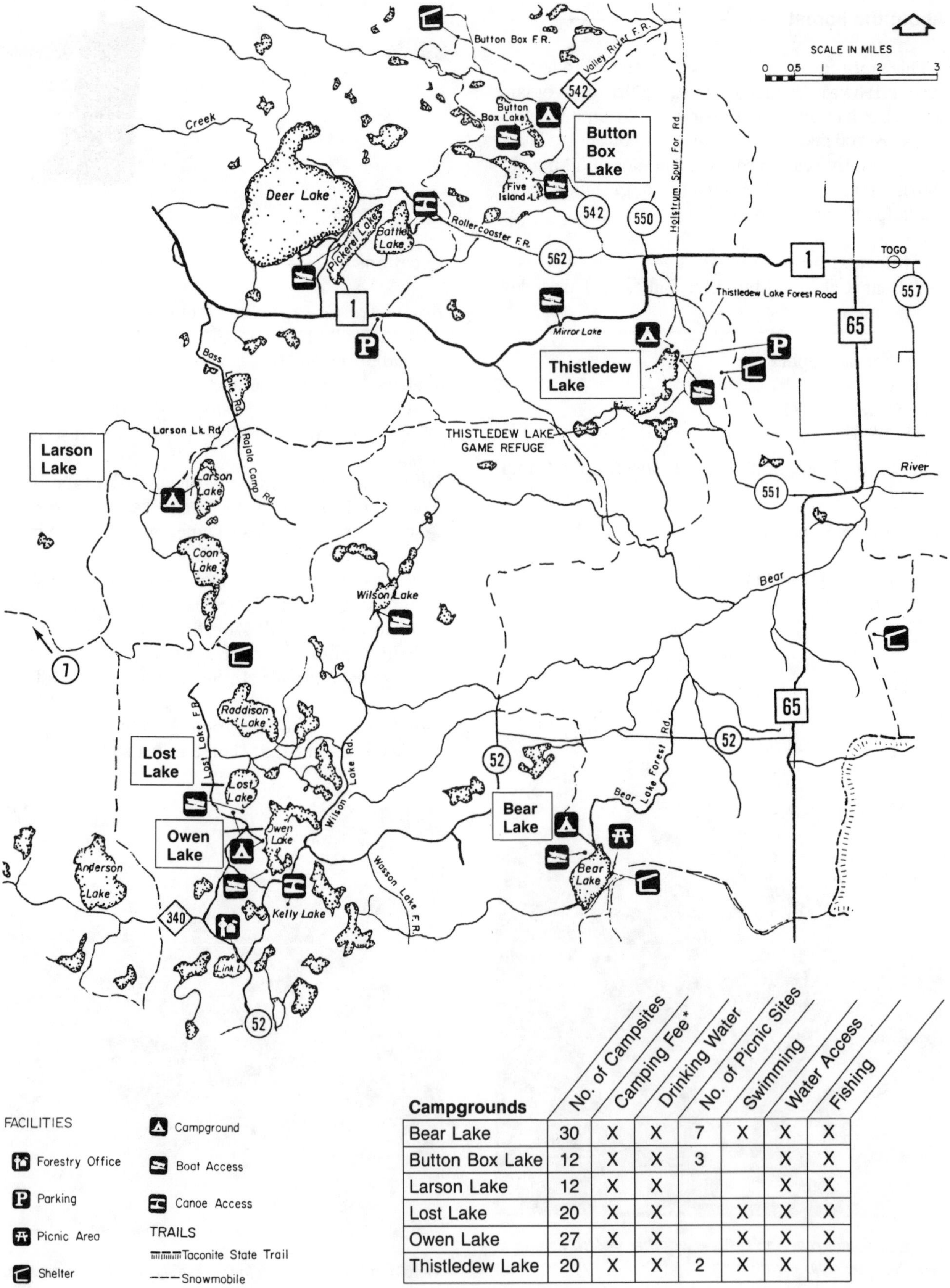

FACILITIES

- Forestry Office
- Parking
- Picnic Area
- Shelter
- Campground
- Boat Access
- Canoe Access

TRAILS

- Taconite State Trail
- Snowmobile

Campgrounds	No. of Campsites	Camping Fee*	Drinking Water	No. of Picnic Sites	Swimming	Water Access	Fishing
Bear Lake	30	X	X	7	X	X	X
Button Box Lake	12	X	X	3		X	X
Larson Lake	12	X	X			X	X
Lost Lake	20	X	X		X	X	X
Owen Lake	27	X	X		X	X	X
Thistledew Lake	20	X	X	2	X	X	X

Gooseberry Falls State Park

For Information

Gooseberry Falls State Park
1300 Highway 61 East
Two Harbors, MN 55616
(218) 834-3855

Location

Gooseberry Falls State Park is located in Lake County in Minnesota's North Shore highlands 12 miles northeast of Two Harbors on US 61. The rocky Lake Superior shoreline and 5 waterfalls highlight this 1,662-acre park. The Gooseberry River meanders into the park to finish its journey to Lake Superior. The best waterfalls are at the Highway 61 bridge. The water tumbles over the Upper Falls 30 feet into the pool, glides to the two-tiered Lower Falls, and plunges 60 feet into the last pool.

Facilities & Activities

72 drive-in campsites
3 walk-in campsites
dump station
flush toilets (H)
vault toilets (H)
winterized showers (H)
rustic group camp
picnic area with enclosed shelter
fishing (stream & lake)
visitor center (seasonal)
interpretive program (seasonal)
winter access
warming house
18 miles of foot trails
1.5 miles of self-guided trails
12 miles of X-country ski trails
2 miles of snowmobile trails (embarkation point & connecting link to North Shore Trail)

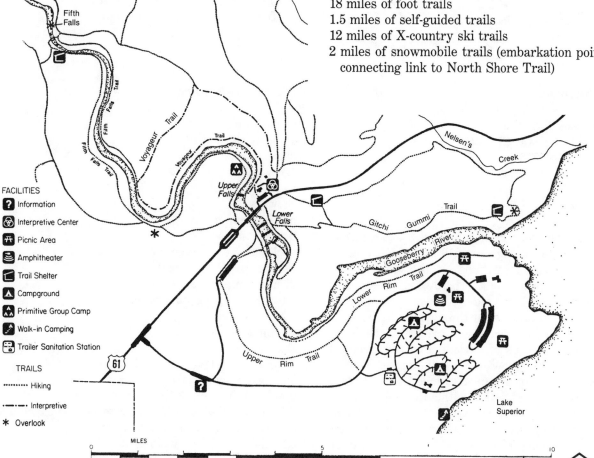

FACILITIES

? Information

Interpretive Center

Picnic Area

Amphitheater

Trail Shelter

Campground

Primitive Group Camp

Walk-in Camping

Trailer Sanitation Station

TRAILS

········· Hiking

—·—·— Interpretive

✳ Overlook

Jay Cooke State Park

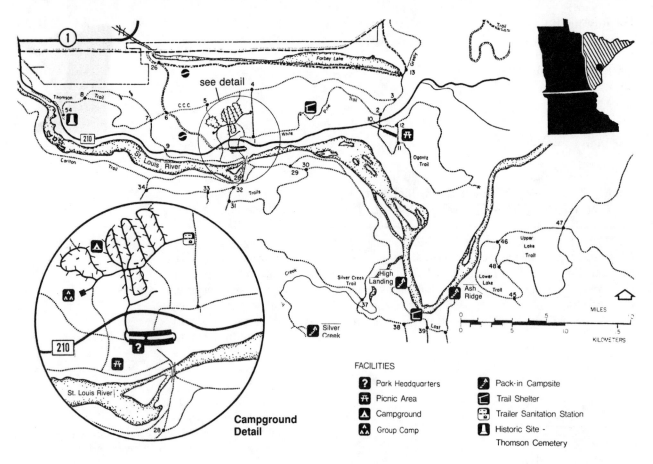

Campground
Detail

FACILITIES

? Park Headquarters	**♦** Pack-in Campsite
⊼ Picnic Area	**⚑** Trail Shelter
▲ Campground	**⊞** Trailer Sanitation Station
⚏ Group Camp	**⚏** Historic Site – Thomson Cemetery

For Information

Jay Cooke State Park
500 East Highway 210
Carlton, MN 55718
(218) 384-4610

Location

Jay Cooke State Park is located 3 miles east of Carlton on State Highway 210 in Carlton County. The rugged land formations of this 8,813-acre park enhance the beauty of the hardwood forests. The water-eroded gorge, steep valleys, and massive rock formations are seen throughout the park. In some seasons, the waters of the St. Louis River thunder over slabs of ancient, exposed rock. At other times, they slow to a gentle trickle. Four of the 19 poses or pauses of the 7-mile Grand Portage of the St. Louis River are within the boundaries of the park. This portage, used up to 1870, served as the connecting link between two great drainage systems—the upper Mississippi River and Lake Superior.

Facilities & Activities

80 drive-in campsites
4 backpack campsites
dump station
flush toilets
vault toilets (H)
showers
rustic group camp
2 picnic areas
enclosed & open shelters
fishing (river)
visitor center (year-round)
interpretive program (seasonal)
winter access
warming house
snacks
historic site—Thompson cemetery
50 miles of foot trails
5 miles of horseback riding trails
5.5 miles of bike trails & access to 14-mile paved bicycle trail from Carlton to Duluth
32 miles of X-country ski trails
12 miles of snowmobile trails

Judge C. R. Magney State Park

For Information

Judge C. R. Magney State Park
Box 500, East Star Route
Grand Marais, MN 55604
(218) 387-2929

Location

Judge C. R. Magney State Park is located in Cook County, 14 miles northeast of Grand Marais on U.S. 61. The 4,514-acre park, located on the Brule River, is named in honor of the former mayor of Duluth and district court judge who helped establish 11 state parks and waysides along the North Shore.

About the Park

The scenic Brule River races through the park, forming whitewater rapids and waterfalls on its way to Lake Superior. Along the lower stretches of the river, within 2 miles of Lake Superior, is a series of spectacular waterfalls. Here you can find the mysterious Devil's Kettle Falls. Above the Devil's Kettle, a jutting rock mass divides the river into 2 sections. The eastern section drops about 50 feet to a pool below, while the western portion plunges into a huge pothole and, according to local legend, disappears forever.

FACILITIES

? Information

🏕 Picnic Area

⛺ Campground

TRAILS

········ Hiking

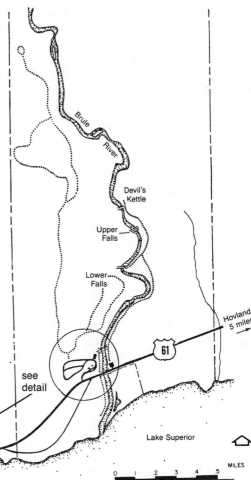

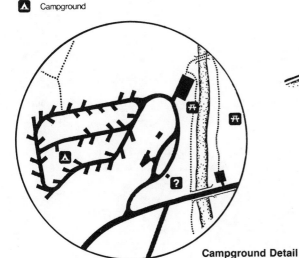

Campground Detail

Facilities & Activities

36 drive-in rustic campsites
vault toilets
picnic area
fishing (lake & river)
winter access
6 miles of foot trails
5 miles of X-country ski trails

Kabetogama State Forest

For Information

Area Forest Supervisor
Orr, MN 55771
(218) 757-3274

About the Forest

The Kabetogama State Forest contains many lakes of different sizes from the small 10-acre class to one of the largest lakes in Minnesota—Lake Vermilion. The forest borders on the Boundary Waters Canoe Area where numerous canoe routes are managed. Outdoor recreational facilities include the Ash River, Hinsdale Island (boat-in only), Wakemup Bay and Wooden Frog campgrounds, the 12.5-mile Ash River Ski Touring and Hiking Trail, and the 68-mile Pelican Lake area snowmobile trails.

Location

Ash River Campground—From Orr, take US 53 north 26 miles to CR 126 (Ash River Road); turn right and travel 9 miles east.

Wakemup Bay Campground—From Cook, take CR 24 2.5 miles north to CR 78; turn right (east) & travel 3 miles; then left (north) for 1 mile.

Wooden Frog Campground—From Orr, take US 53 north for 30 miles to CR 122; turn right (north) and follow signs about 6 miles.

For those camping in the forest, the early morning fog has a certain mystique about it.

Campgrounds	No. of Campsites	Camping Fee	Drinking Water	No. of Picnic Sites	Swimming	Water Access	Fishing
Ash River	9	X	X	2		X	X
Wakemup Bay	21	X	X	2	X	X	X
Wooden Frog	59	X	X	10	X	X	X

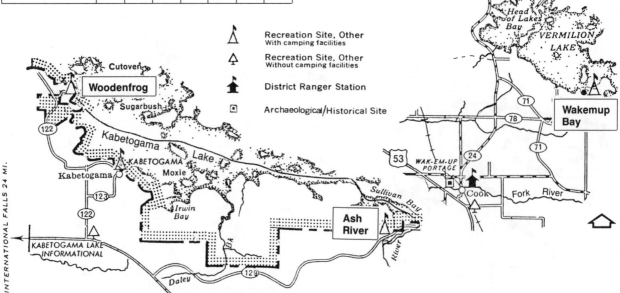

Recreation Site, Other
With camping facilities

Recreation Site, Other
Without camping facilities

District Ranger Station

Archaeological/Historical Site

McCarthy Beach State Park

FACILITIES

? Information

🏕 Trail Shelter

🏖 Beach

🚤 Boat Ramp

🏕 Campground

🏠 Ranger Station

🗼 Lookout Tower

🚻 Trailer Sanitation Station

TRAILS

— — — Taconite State Trail

·········· Hiking

⑤ Numbered Trail Intersection

These campers are well prepared; the canopy offers protection from the sun as well as a sudden shower.

For Information

McCarthy Beach State Park
HCR 5, Box 341
Hibbing, MN 55746
(218) 254-2411

Location

McCarthy Beach State Park is located in St. Louis County near Hibbing. Take US 169 north out of Hibbing to County Road 5. Follow this county road 15 miles north to the park entrance. McCarthy Beach offers excellent water and land recreation. The 2,566-acre park is between 2 major lakes, Sturgeon Lake and Side Lake. In and around the park, 5 additional lakes provide opportunities to fish for trout, walleye, and panfish. The park's terrain is that of rolling hills with many small valleys.

Facilities & Activities

45 drive-in modern campsites
14 drive-in primitive campsites
dump station

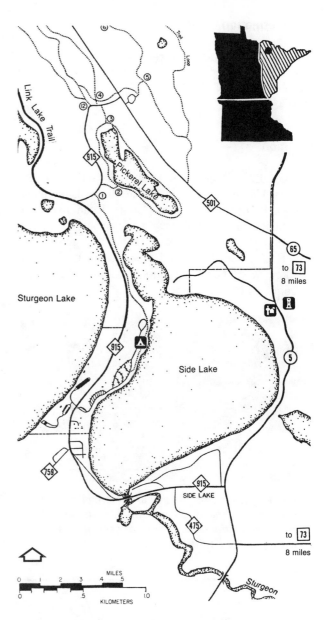

flush toilets (H)
vault toilets (H)
showers (H)
picnic area with enclosed shelter (H)
swimming
fishing (lake)
boat launch
lake access
interpretive program (seasonal)
winter access
warming house
11 miles of foot trails
5 miles of X-country ski trails
12 miles of snowmobile trails

Moose Lake Recreation Area

For Information

Moose Lake Recreation Area
1000 County 137
Moose Lake, MN 55767
(218) 485-4059

Location

Moose Lake Recreation Area is located in Carlton County 1 mile east of I-35 at the Moose Lake exit. The park entrance is off of County Road 137. The popularity of this 965-acre park arises from its sandy beach, wooded hiking trails, and good fishing. Both lakes, Echo and Moosehead, have been stocked with northern pike, walleye pike, and largemouth bass.

*If your destination was Moose Lake Recreation Area . . .
slow down . . . 'cause you're there! All state parks have
large signs, so there's no chance of passing one by . . .
assuming you're on the right road!*

Facilities & Activities

18 drive-in rustic campsites
vault toilets (H)
picnic area with shelter (H)
swimming beach
fishing (lake)
boat launch
boat & canoe rental
winter access
4 miles of foot trails
5 miles of X-country ski trails
5 miles of snowmobile trails

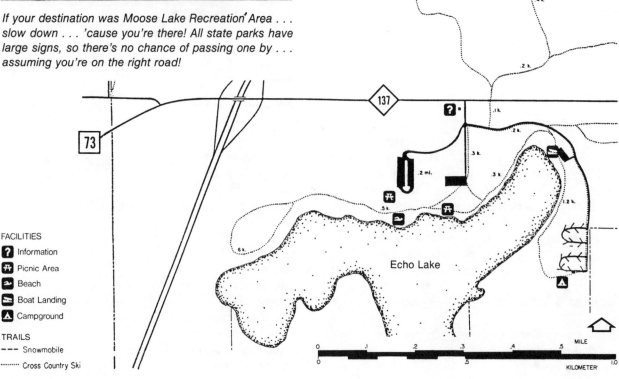

FACILITIES
❓ Information
🏕 Picnic Area
🏖 Beach
🚣 Boat Landing
⛺ Campground

TRAILS
--- Snowmobile
········· Cross Country Ski

Echo Lake

MILE

KILOMETER

Nemadji State Forest
(Gafvert Campground)

For Information

Area Forest Supervisor
Route 2, 701 South Kenwood
Moose Lake, MN 55767
(218) 485-4474

Location

On Pickerel Lake. Go 1 mile north from Nickerson on SH 23; turn right (south) ¼ mile, then east 1 mile on CR 145; turn right (south) on Net Lake FR for 1.5 miles to Pickerel Lake.

Facilities

9 campsites
fee area
drinking water
1 picnic site
water access
fishing
access to 68 miles of multi-purpose trails

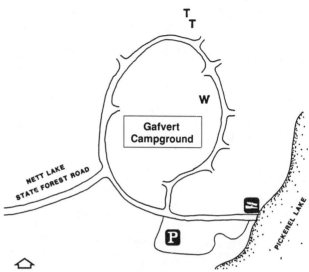

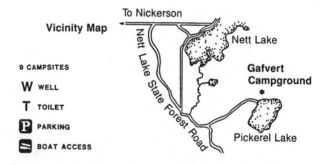

Vicinity Map

9 CAMPSITES
W WELL
T TOILET
P PARKING
≋ BOAT ACCESS

The wife decided to sleep late this foggy morning . . .

. . . and judging from the stern-heavy canoe, her absence is quite noticeable!

St. Croix State Forest

About the Forest

Outdoor recreation facilities in the St. Croix State Forest include Boulder Campground, Tamarack River Equestrian Camp, a portion of the Minnesota-Wisconsin Boundary Trail, and trails for hiking, horseback riding, and snowmobiling. The map/brochure also shows the location of 8 primitive campsites along the trails.

For Information

Area Forest Supervisor
Route 2, 701 South Kenwood
Moose Lake, MN 55767
(218) 485-4474

Location

On Rock Lake. Travel SH 123 east from Sandstone to CR 30; continue east 14 miles to Duxbury; turn right (south) on CR 24 for 2 miles; turn left (east) on CR 25 for 4 miles; turn right (south) on CR 173 for ¾-mile; turn left (east) on Tamarack State Forest Road and follow signs.

Facilities

19 campsites
fee area
drinking water
6 picnic sites
water access
fishing
horse corral

Vicinity Map

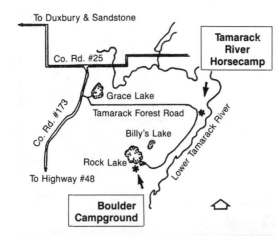

With these large windows, this family tent should be fairly comfortable on even the warmest of days.

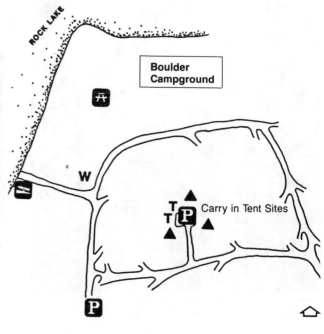

St. Croix State Park

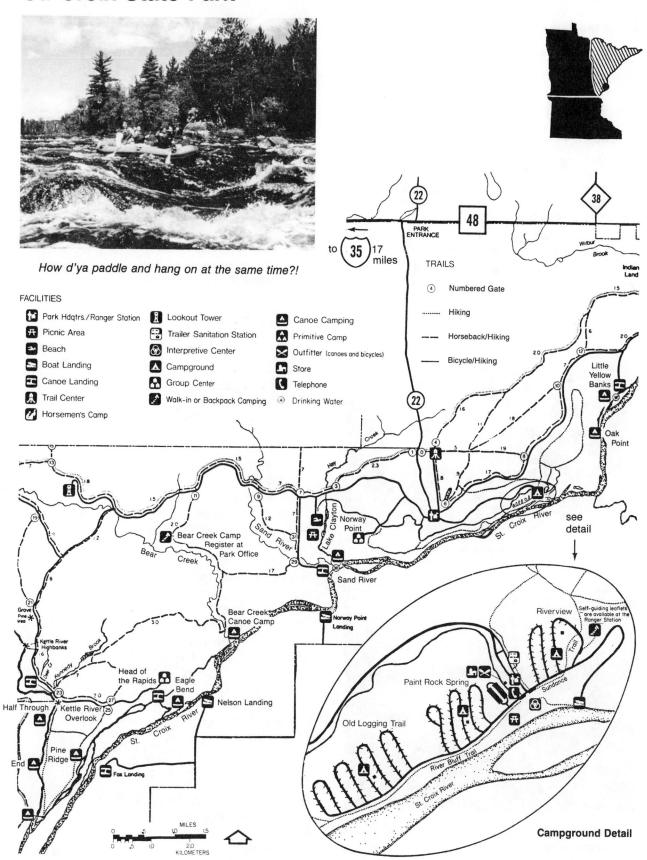

How d'ya paddle and hang on at the same time?!

FACILITIES

- 🏠 Park Hdqtrs./Ranger Station
- 🏕 Picnic Area
- 🏊 Beach
- 🚤 Boat Landing
- 🛶 Canoe Landing
- 🥾 Trail Center
- 🐴 Horsemen's Camp
- 🔭 Lookout Tower
- 🚻 Trailer Sanitation Station
- ⊙ Interpretive Center
- ⛺ Campground
- 👥 Group Center
- 🎒 Walk-in or Backpack Camping
- ⛺ Canoe Camping
- 🏕 Primitive Camp
- ✂ Outfitter (canoes and bicycles)
- 🏪 Store
- ☎ Telephone
- Ⓦ Drinking Water

TRAILS

- ④ Numbered Gate
- .... Hiking
- – – – Horseback/Hiking
- ——— Bicycle/Hiking

to 🄴35 17 miles

PARK ENTRANCE

Wilbur Brook

Indian Land

Little Yellow Banks

Oak Point

see detail

Creek

Bear Creek Camp Register at Park Office

Bear Creek

Sand River

Lake Clayton

Norway Point

Sand River

Bear Creek Canoe Camp

Norway Point Landing

Grove Pine Area

Kettle River Highbanks

Head of the Rapids

Eagle Bend

Nelson Landing

Half Through

Kettle River Overlook

Pine Ridge

End

Fox Landing

St. Croix River

MILES
KILOMETERS

Campground Detail

Riverview

Self-guiding leaflets are available at the Ranger Station

Paint Rock Spring

Sundance Trail

Old Logging Trail

River Bluff Trail

St. Croix River

St. Croix State Park *(continued)*

For Information

St. Croix State Park
Route 3, Box 174
Hinckley, MN 55037
(612) 384-6591

Location

St. Croix State Park is located in Pine County 16 miles east of Hinckley on State Highway 48. The park headquarters is on County Road 22, 5 miles south of the park entrance. St. Croix is the largest state park in Minnesota, containing over 33,000 acres of forests, meadows, marshes, and streams. The St. Croix River adjoining the park has been designated a National Wild and Scenic River. Seven miles of the Kettle River, a Minnesota Wild and Scenic River, form the western boundary of the park.

Campsites at state parks include a picnic table and grill; . . .

. . . and water-oriented parks usually have a boat launch as well as a boat dock.

The park rents canoes and provides a canoe shuttle service for excursions on the St. Croix River.

Facilities & Activities

213 drive-in campsites
4 walk-in campsites
2 backpack campsites
10 canoe campsites
42 campsites with electricity
dump station
flush toilets (H)
vault toilets (H)
showers (H)
horse camping
3 modern group camps (395 total capacity)
rustic group camp (200 capacity)
picnic area with 2 enclosed shelters (H)
swimming beach on Lake Clayton
fishing (river & stream)
boat launch
6 canoe landings
canoe & bicycle rental
visitor center (seasonal)
interpretive program (seasonal)
all-seasons trail center
winter access
warming house
snacks/groceries
lookout tower
canoe shuttle
127 miles of foot trails
1 mile of self-guided trail
75 miles of horseback riding trails
6 miles of surfaced bike trails
21 miles of X-country ski trails
75 miles of snowmobile trails

Sandy Lake Recreation Area

Statistics

9,400 acres in size

77 miles of shoreline

421 square-mile drainage area runoff (including 8 lakes) controlled by dam

120-acre recreation area

operated & maintained by U.S. Army Corps of Engineers, St. Paul District

Resource Manager's Office

Sandy Lake Recreation Area
Route 4
McGregor, MN 57760
(218) 426-3482

Facilities

49 camping sites
18 sites with electricity
drinking water
showers
restrooms
trailer dump station
picnic area/day use area
playground
game area
swimming area
boat ramp
canoe launch
interpretive display
handicapped facilities
no reservations accepted

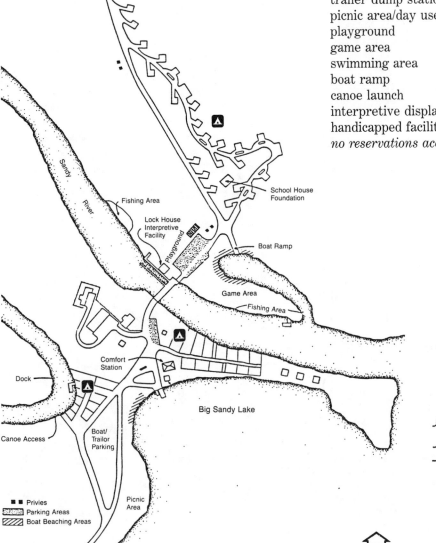

Sandy River

Fishing Area

Lock House Interpretive Facility

Playground

School House Foundation

Boat Ramp

Game Area

Fishing Area

Comfort Station

Dock

Canoe Access

Boat/ Trailor Parking

Big Sandy Lake

Picnic Area

■ ■ Privies
▨ Parking Areas
▨ Boat Beaching Areas

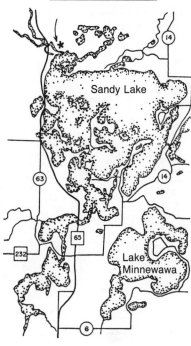

Sandy Lake Dam & Recreation Areas

Sandy Lake

Lake Minnewawa

14

63

65

232

6

Savanna Portage State Park

For Information

Savanna Portage State Park
HCR 3, Box 591
McGregor, MN 55760
(218) 426-3271

Location

Savanna Portage State Park is located in Aitkin County 17 miles northeast of McGregor. Take US 65 to County Road 14 and County Road 36 the 10 miles to the park entrance. Savanna Portage State Park has 15,818 acres of rolling hills, lakes, and bogs. The Savanna Portage was a vital link between the St. Louis River watershed and that of the Mississippi River on the canoe route from Lake Superior to the Upper Mississippi. Savanna, meaning open grassland, refers to the expanse of marsh grass on the eastern portion of the trail. Before the white man, this 6-mile portage was used for centuries by the native North Americans.

Facilities & Activities

60 drive-in campsites
6 backpack campsites
dump station
flush toilets (H)
vault toilets (H)
showers
rustic group camp
picnic area with shelter (H)
swimming
fishing (lake)

boat launch & boat access (carry)
boat & canoe rental
winter access
warming house
historic site—Savanna Portage trail
motor rental
boat motor restrictions
22 miles of foot trails
10 miles of mountain bike trails
16 miles of X-country ski trails
61 miles of snowmobile trails

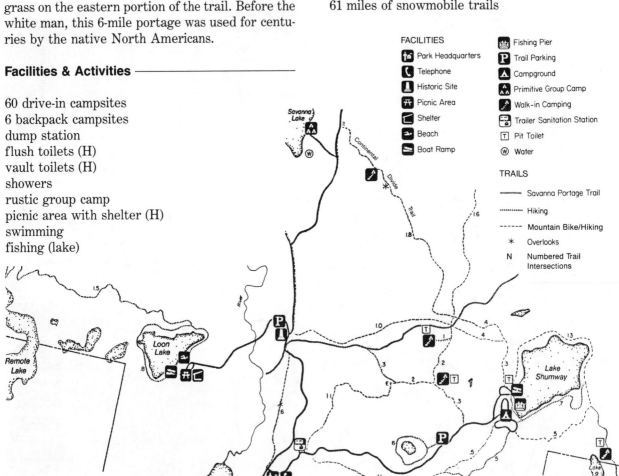

FACILITIES

	Park Headquarters
	Telephone
	Historic Site
	Picnic Area
	Shelter
	Beach
	Boat Ramp

	Fishing Pier
	Trail Parking
	Campground
	Primitive Group Camp
	Walk-in Camping
	Trailer Sanitation Station
	Pit Toilet
	Water

TRAILS

Savanna Portage Trail
Hiking
Mountain Bike/Hiking
* Overlooks
N Numbered Trail Intersections

Savanna State Forest

(Hay Lake Campground)

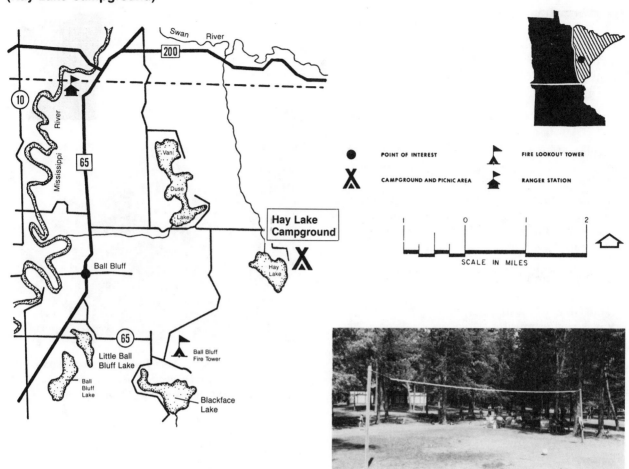

Point of Interest

Campground and Picnic Area

Fire Lookout Tower

Ranger Station

SCALE IN MILES

For Information

Area Forest Supervisor
Box 9
Hill City, MN 55748
(218) 697-2476

Location

From Jacobson, take SH 65 south for 2.5 miles; turn left (east) for 3 miles, then south for 1 mile.

Facilities & Activities

20 campsites
fee area
drinking water
10 picnic sites
swimming
water access
fishing
hiking trail
access to 34 miles of snowmobile trails

Picnic areas at many parks offer recreational activities; these areas are ideal for group gatherings.

Park Rangers are available at the Visitor Centers to help you plan your trip to this water-dominated park.

Scenic State Park

For Information

Scenic State Park
Bigfork, MN 56628
(218) 743-3363

Location

Scenic State Park is located in Itasca County, 7 miles east of State Highway 38 at Bigfork on County Road 7. The park protects the entire virgin pine shorelands of Coon and Sandwick Lakes, plus parts of 4 other lakes. The 2,922-acre park contains several magnificent stands of old white and red pine that visitors enjoy walking through.

Facilities & Activities

120 drive-in campsites
12 backpack campsites
7 canoe campsites
20 campsites with electricity
dump station
flush toilets (H)
vault toilets (H)
showers (H)
rustic group camp
picnic area with enclosed shelter (H)
swimming
fishing (lake)
boat launch & boat access (carry)
boat & canoe rental
visitor center (seasonal)
interpretive program (seasonal)
winter access
warming house
lookout fire tower
10 miles of foot trails
5 miles of self-guided trails
5 miles of mountain bike trails
10 miles of X-country ski trails
10 miles of snowmobile trails

Loon Lake, at Scenic State Park, offers great opportunities for boating and fishing. This boat driver needed a steady hand to maneuver into this parking spot.

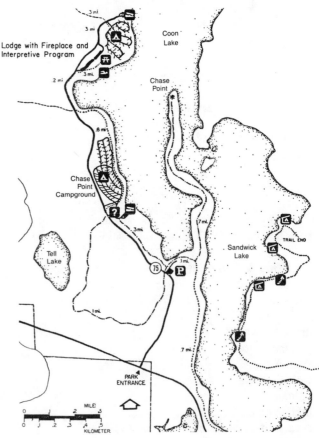

FACILITIES		TRAILS
? Information	A Campground	⋯⋯ Hiking
Picnic Area	Primitive Group Camp	--- Mountain Bike / Hiking
Boat Landing	Walk-in Campsite	— Interpretive
Swimming Beach	Shelter-Campsite	
	P Parking	

Split Rock Lighthouse State Park

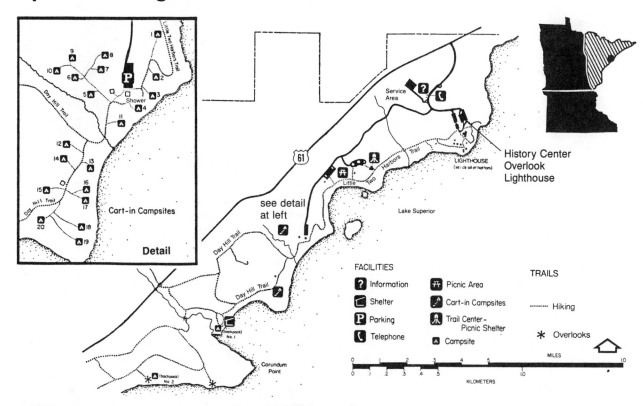

FACILITIES

? Information	**↗** Picnic Area		
◿ Shelter	**△** Cart-in Campsites		
P Parking	**◮** Trail Center–Picnic Shelter		
☎ Telephone	**△** Campsite		

TRAILS

········· Hiking

* Overlooks

History Center
Overlook
Lighthouse

Split Rock Lighthouse, completed in 1910, is probably the most visited lighthouse in the United States.

Facilities & Activities

20 cart-in campsites
4 backpack campsites
flush toilets (H)
vault toilets (H)
showers (H)
picnic area with enclosed and open shelters (H)
fishing (stream & lake)
trail center (year-round)
winter access
historic site—Split Rock Lighthouse
8 miles of foot trails
8 miles of X-country ski trails

For Information

Split Rock Lighthouse State Park
2010A Highway 61 East
Two Harbors, MN 55616

Location

Split Rock Lighthouse State Park is located in
Lake County about 20 miles northeast of Two Harbors on US 61. The Minnesota Historical Society
administers the 25-acre Split Rock Lighthouse Historic Site and the recently completed history center
adjacent to the site. Decommissioned by the Coast
Guard in 1969, Split Rock Lighthouse operated for
59 years over Western Lake Superior.

This 1,872-acre park, located on magnificent
bluffs on the North Shore, is the home of Minnesota
state park's first cart-in campground—a walk-in
campground for tenters. Campers park their vehicles in the campground parking lot, load their gear
into lightweight carts, then wheel their gear down
gravel trails to preselected campsites. The walking
distance in can vary between 350 and 1950 feet, depending on which campsite is selected.

Superior National Forest

For Information

Forest Supervisor
Superior National Forest
P.O. Box 338
Duluth, MN 55801
(218) 720-5324

About the Forest

The Superior National Forest encompasses more than 3 million acres of lakes and streams, deep evergreen forests, and stark outcroppings of weathered granite. The landscape testifies to the passage of hundreds of millions of years during which volcanic activity, warm inland seas, and glaciers each took its turn as architect.

In the northern portion of the forest is the only canoe wilderness in the United States—the Boundary Waters Canoe Area (BWCA). It is governed by special regulations, which can be obtained by writing to the forest supervisor in Duluth.

Duluth, headquarters for the Superior National Forest, lies 60 miles south of the forest. Three major highways offer easy access to the forest from Duluth—US 61 runs along the north shore of Lake Superior to the Forest's eastern edge; US 53 travels north to the western portion of the forest; and SH 169 runs northeast from Virginia to Ely in the center of the forest.

Camping opportunities in the Superior National Forest range from fully developed campgrounds to secluded sites with few or no facilities. Most campgrounds are open from spring through late fall. Usually, at least one campground in each area is open during the off-season, but roads are often unplowed, limiting access.

Most campgrounds have a fireplace, table, tent pad, and a parking spur that accommodates trailers up to 22 feet long. Some units are designed as carry-in tent sites. Fall Lake Campground has cold running water, flush toilets, and a trailer dumping station, but all other campgrounds are more rustic in nature with hand pumps and pit toilets. Daily

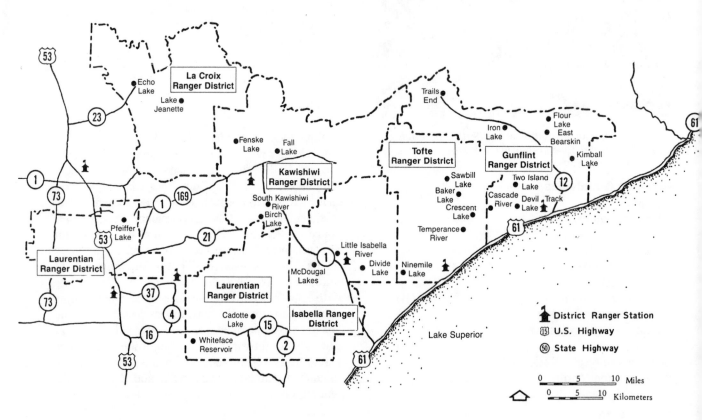

Superior National Forest *(continued)*

fees at developed campgrounds help cover operation and maintenance costs. Many campgrounds have unsupervised swimming beaches, boat landings, and interpretive trails. Pets are allowed, but must be kept under control.

For those preferring a more solitary experience, the forest offers over 200 individual, primitive campsites outside the BWCA. While many are accessible by water only, others can be reached by foot or vehicle. Contact the appropriate ranger district office for help in locating these sites. In addition, many sites throughout the forest have no latrines, firegrates, or other improvements. This type of primitive camping carries the special responsibility of leaving the area in a natural state so those who follow cannot tell the site has been used.

More than 2,000 lakes and a network of streams and rivers are found in the Superior National Forest. Motor use and size are restricted in the BWCA, but in the rest of the forest boating and canoeing opportunities are endless. There are 12 primitive canoe routes outside the BWCA. The Forest Service maintains over 30 boat launch sites in addition to those providing access to the BWCA. These launch sites range from paved lots and ramp access to those where boats and canoes must be carried down to the water.

Forest hiking trails varying in length and difficulty provide an adventure of a few hours, a day, overnight, or even a week or more. Trail maps, as well as a Recreation Trail Index that displays trails by type (hiking, X-country skiing, snowmobiling), length, location, and facilities, are available at ranger district offices.

Northwood winters are ideally suited to winter sports—X-country skiing and downhill skiing, snowmobiling, camping, snowshoeing, ice fishing, skating, and sledding. The Superior National Forest is large enough to accommodate all of these activities, but in some areas those traveling by skis, snowshoes, or snowmobiles must share the same route. Common sense and courtesy enable everyone to enjoy a safe and pleasant experience.

Designated trails are listed in the *Recreation Trail Index*, but many miles of unplowed roads also are open to winter travel. You may wish to combine your travel with winter camping. Most areas in the National Forest are open to camping, but be aware that camping is prohibited in day-use areas such as parking lots, boat landings, and picnic grounds.

Gunflint Ranger District

For Information

Gunflint Ranger District
Superior National Forest
Grand Marais, MN 55604
(218) 387-1750

Campground Locations

Cascade River Campground—.5 mile north from Grand Marais on CR 12 (Gunflint Trail), 4 miles west on CR 7, 9 miles northwest on FR 158.

Devil Track Lake Campground—3.7 miles north from Grand Marais on CR 12 (Gunflint Trail), 1 mile west and 5 miles north on CR 8, 2.5 miles west on CR 57.

East Bearskin Lake Campground—25 miles north from Grand Marais on CR 12 (Gunflint Trail), 1.5 miles northeast on FR 146.

Flour Lake Campground—27 miles north from Grand Marais on CR 12 (Gunflint Trail), 3 miles northeast on CR 66.

Iron Lake Campground—36 miles north from Grand Marais on CR 12 (Gunflint Trail), 2 miles west on CR 92.

Kimball Lake Campground—10.7 miles northeast from Grand Marais on CR 12 (Gunflint Trail), 2 miles east on FR 140.

Trails End Campground—57 miles northwest from Grand Marais on CR 12 (Gunflint Trail) to the end of the Gunflint Trail.

Two Island Lake Campground—3.7 miles north from Grand Marais on CR 12 (Gunflint Trail), 1 mile west and 5 miles north on CR 8, 4 miles northwest on CR 27.

Superior National Forest *(continued)*

Developed Campgrounds	No. of Camping Units*	Toilets	Drinking Water	Picnic Area[2]	Trailer Space	Swimming	Boat Landing
Cascade River	3	X	X[1]		X		
Devil Track Lake	16*	X	X	X	X		C
East Bearskin Lake	33*	X	X	X	X		X
Flour Lake	35*	X	X	X	X		X
Iron Lake	7	X	X	X	X		C
Kimball Lake	8*	X	X	X	X		X
Trails End	33*	X	X	X	X	X	X
Two Island River	36*	X	X	X	X		X

* Accessible to the handicapped
C Carry-down access
[1] Spring water, tested annually
[2] No designated picnic area but picnicking is allowed
Note: Contact the district ranger for locations of the 28 dispersed campsites accessible by canoe and boat.

Cascade River Campground

Devil Track Lake Campground

East Bearskin Lake Campground

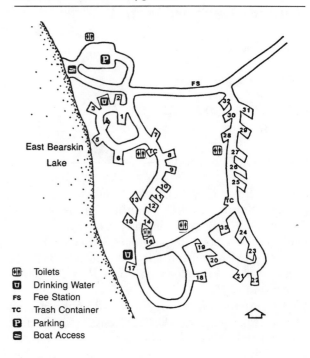

The Superior National Forest offer countless opportunities for canoeing, including the Boundary Waters Canoe Area in the northern portion—the only canoe wilderness in the United States (pages 23–25).

Superior National Forest *(continued)*

Flour Lake Campground

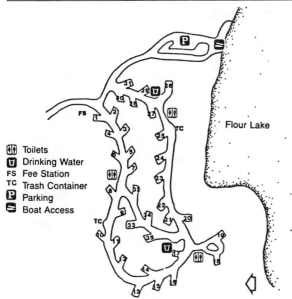

Flour Lake

Toilets
Drinking Water
FS Fee Station
TC Trash Container
P Parking
Boat Access

Trails End Campground

Gunflint Trail

Granol Marais
57 miles

Gull Lake

Seagull Lake

Toilets
Drinking Water
FS Fee Station
TC Trash Container
P Parking
Boat Access
Picnicking
Gasoline
Groceries
Telephone

Iron Lake Campground

CR 92

Forest Road #150

FS

Iron Lake

Toilets
Drinking Water
FS Fee Station
TC Trash Container
Carry Down Access

Two Island River Campground

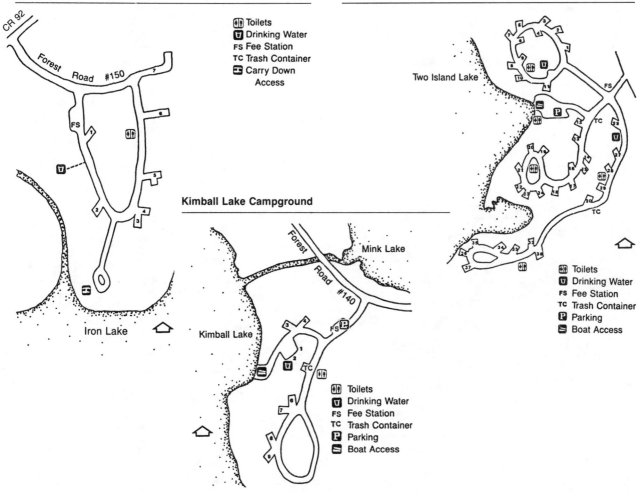

Two Island Lake

Toilets
Drinking Water
FS Fee Station
TC Trash Container
P Parking
Boat Access

Kimball Lake Campground

Forest Road #140

Mink Lake

Kimball Lake

FS
P

Toilets
Drinking Water
FS Fee Station
TC Trash Container
P Parking
Boat Access

Superior National Forest *(continued)*

Isabella Ranger District

For Information

Isabella Ranger District
Superior National Forest
2759 Highway 1
Isabella, MN 55607
(218) 323-7722

Campground Locations

Divide Lake Campground—5 miles east from Isabella on FR 172.
Little Isabella River Campground—4.5 miles west from Isabella on SH 1.
McDougal Lake Campground—10 miles west from Isabella on SH 1, then .5 mile south on FR 106.

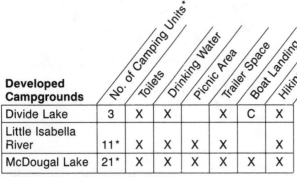

Developed Campgrounds	No. of Camping Units*	Toilets	Drinking Water	Picnic Area	Trailer Space	Boat Landing	Hiking Trail
Divide Lake	3	X	X		X	C	X
Little Isabella River	11*	X	X	X	X		X
McDougal Lake	21*	X	X	X	X	X	X

* Accessible to the handicapped
C Carry-down access
Note: Contact the district ranger for locations of the 58 dispersed campsites accessible by road, canoe or trail.
Swimming is featured at McDougal Lake.

Divide Lake Campground

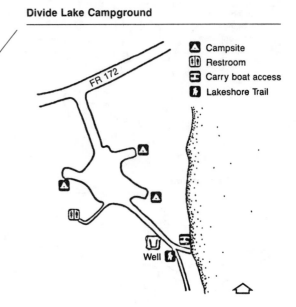

- 🄰 Campsite
- 🚻 Restroom
- 🛶 Carry boat access
- 🚶 Lakeshore Trail

Little Isabella River Campground

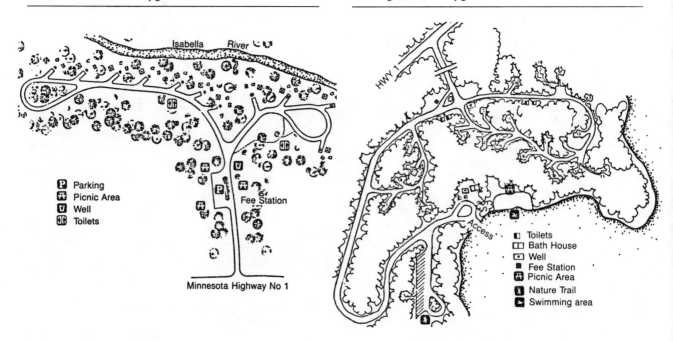

- 🅿 Parking
- 🛉 Picnic Area
- Ⓤ Well
- 🚻 Toilets

Minnesota Highway No 1

McDougal Lake Campground

- 🚻 Toilets
- 🛁 Bath House
- Ⓤ Well
- ▪ Fee Station
- 🛉 Picnic Area
- 🚶 Nature Trail
- 🏊 Swimming area

Superior National Forest *(continued)*

Kawishiwi Ranger District

For Information

Kawishiwi Ranger District
Superior National Forest
118 South 4th Ave. East
Ely, MN 55731
(218) 365-6185

Campground Locations

Birch Lake Campground—8 miles south from Ely on SH 1, 4 miles south on FR 429.
Fall Lake Campground—6 miles east from Ely on SH 169/CR 18, 1 mile northeast on FR 551.
Fenske Lake Campground—1.5 miles east from Ely on SH 169, 2.4 miles north on CR 88, 7 miles north on CR 116 (Echo Trail).
South Kawishiwi River Campground—10 miles south from Ely on SH 1.

Developed Campgrounds	No. of Camping Units*	Toilets	Drinking Water	Picnic Area	Trailer Space	Swimming	Boat Landing
Birch Lake[1]	32	X	X		X		X
Fall Lake	67*	X	X	X	X	X	X
Fenske Lake[2]	16*	X	X	X	X	X	X
South Kawishiwi River[3]	32*	X	X	X	X	X	X

* Accessible to the handicapped
[1] 2 loops, each with 16 sites; only 1 loop open at a time except during peak use periods
[2] Has an open log pavillion
[3] Has an enclosed log pavillion with fireplace, available for rental
There are hiking trails at Fenske Lake and South Kawishiwi River.

Fall Lake Campground

- Toilets–Flush & Vault
- Dump Station
- Parking
- Boat Access
- Picnic Area
- Swimming
- TC Trash Container

Birch Lake Campground

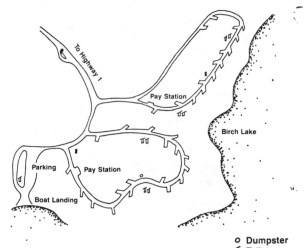

- o Dumpster
- Toilet
- Well

Minnesota is known for its 10,000 lakes, but that doesn't mean an absence of fast-flowing rivers!

REGION 2

Superior National Forest (continued)

Fenske Lake Campground

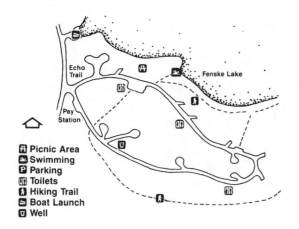

- 🏕 Picnic Area
- 🏊 Swimming
- 🅿 Parking
- 🚻 Toilets
- 🚶 Hiking Trail
- ⛴ Boat Launch
- 💧 Well

South Kawishiwi River Campground

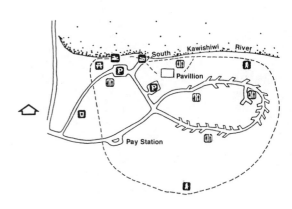

La Croix Ranger District

For Information

La Croix Ranger District
Superior National Forest
P.O. Box 1085
Cook, MN 55723
(218) 666-5251

Campground Locations

Echo Lake Campground—4 miles north from Buyck on CR 24, 2 miles east on CR 116 (Echo Trail).
Lake Jeanette Campground—4 miles north from Buyck on CR 24, 10 miles east on CR 116 (Echo Trail).

Developed Campgrounds	No. of Camping Units*	Toilets	Drinking Water	Picnic Area	Trailer Space	Swimming	Boat Landing
Echo Lake[1]	24*	X	X	X	X	X	X
Lake Jeanette	9*	X	X		X		X

* Accessible to the handicapped
[1] Includes 1 group campsite
Note: Contact the district ranger for the locations of the 47 dispersed campsites accessible by boat or trail.
There is a hiking trail at Lake Jeanette.

Echo Lake Campground

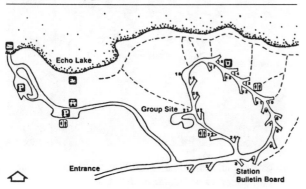

Lake Jeanette Campground

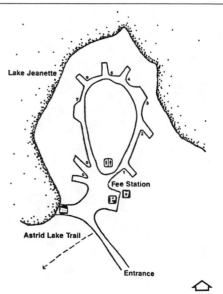

Superior National Forest *(continued)*

Laurentian Ranger District

For Information

Laurentian Ranger District
Superior National Forest
P.O. Box 391
Aurora, MN 55705
(218) 229-3371

Cadotte Lake Campground

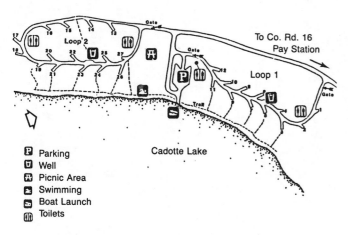

- **P** Parking
- **W** Well
- **Picnic Area**
- **Swimming**
- **Boat Launch**
- **Toilets**

Cadotte Lake

Pfeiffer Lake Campground

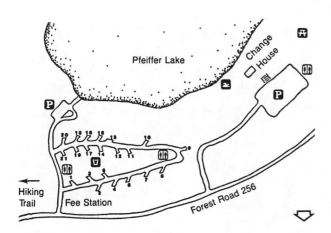

Pfeiffer Lake

Hiking Trail

Fee Station

Forest Road 256

Campground Locations

Cadotte Lake Campground—8 miles north from Rollins on CR 44, 1.5 miles west on CR 16, .4 mile north on FR 425, 1 mile southwest on FR 778.

Pfeiffer Lake Campground—5 miles north from Virginia on US 53, 16 miles northeast on SH 169, 5 miles west on SH 1, 2 miles south on FR 256.

Whiteface Reservoir Campground—5 miles northwest from Markham on CR 4, 6.7 miles east on CR 16, 3 miles south on FR 417.

Whiteface Reservoir Campground

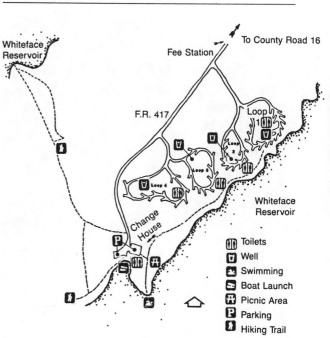

Whiteface Reservoir

To County Road 16

Fee Station

F.R. 417

Loop 1

Whiteface Reservoir

Change House

- **Toilets**
- **Well**
- **Swimming**
- **Boat Launch**
- **Picnic Area**
- **Parking**
- **Hiking Trail**

Developed Campgrounds	No. of Camping Units*	Toilets	Drinking Water	Picnic Area	Trailer Space	Swimming	Boat Landing
Cadotte Lake	27*	X	X	X	X	X	X
Pfeiffer Lake	21*	X	X	X	X	X	X
Whiteface Reservoir[1]	53*	X	X	X	X	X	X

* Accessible to the handicapped
[1] Includes 3 group sites (double sites)
All campgrounds offer hiking trails.

Tofte Ranger District

Crescent Lake Campground

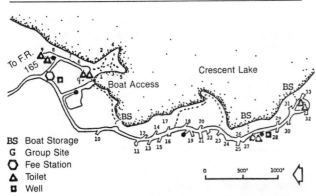

BS Boat Storage
G Group Site
O Fee Station
△ Toilet
◘ Well

The tranquil water of this lake is typical of the lakes in the north woods.

Campground Locations

Baker Lake Campground—.5 mile northeast from Tofte on U.S. 61, 17 miles north on CR 2, 5 miles northeast on CR 165, .5 mile north on FR 1272.

Crescent Lake Campground—.5 mile northeast from Tofte on US 61, 17 miles north on CR 2, 7 miles northeast on FR 165.

Ninemile Lake Campground—.1 mile southwest from Schroeder on US 61, 10 miles west on CR 1 and Lake CR 8, 4 miles north on CR 7.

Sawbill Lake Campground—.5 mile northeast from Tofte on US 61, 24 miles north on CR 2.

Temperance River Campground—.5 mile northeast from Tofte on US 61, 12 miles north on CR 2.

For Information

Tofte Ranger District
Superior National Forest
Tofte, MN 55615
(218) 663-7981

Ninemile Lake Campground

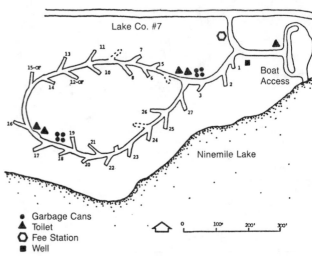

● Garbage Cans
▲ Toilet
O Fee Station
■ Well

. . . "on the road again" . . .

Superior National Forest (continued)

Developed Campgrounds	No. of Camping Units*	Toilets	Drinking Water	Picnic Area	Trailer Space	Boat Landing	Hiking Trail
Baker Lake	5	X	X			X	X
Crescent Lake[1]	33*	X	X		X	X	X
Ninemile Lake	24*	X	X	X	X	X	X
Sawbill Lake	50*	X	X	X	X	C	X
Temperance River	9	X	X		X		

* Accessible to the handicapped
C Carry-down access
[1] Includes 2 group sites, 24 persons each
Established swimming facilities are not offered at any of the campsites.
Note #1: Contact the district ranger for locations of the 22 dispersed campsites accessible by boat or trail.
Note #2: There are also 6 non-fee developed areas for camping that have picnic tables, fire grates and pit toilets, but no approved drinking water or trash containers. These areas are: Kawishiwi Lake Campsite, Lake Clara Campsite, Oxbow Campsite, Poplar River Campsite, Toohey Lake Campsite, and Wilson Lake Campsite.

Temperance River Campground

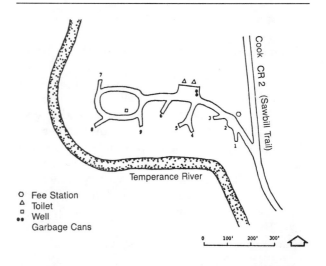

○ Fee Station
△ Toilet
□ Well
•• Well
Garbage Cans

Sawbill Lake Campground

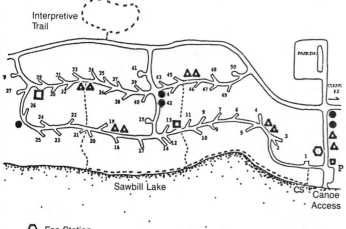

○ Fee Station
△ Toilet
□ Well
P Picnic Area
● Garbage Canister
CS Canoe Storage

Many scenic overlooks along the North Shore provide magnificent views of Lake Superior.

Temperance River State Park

Temperance River State Park
Box 33
Schroeder, MN 55613
(218) 663-7476

Location

Temperance River State Park is located on US 61 in Cook County, just northeast of Schroeder or southwest of Tofte. The 133-acre park is located in a region famous for its bare rock cliffs along the Lake Superior shore. One of the most interesting geologic features in the park is the narrow Temperance River gorge with its many waterfalls. The rapidly falling river cut deep potholes in the soft lava of the river bed. The Ojibwa Indian tribe's name for the river meant "Deep Hollow River." In an 1864 report, Thomas Clark called the stream the Temperance River because unlike other North Shore streams, the river had no bar at its mouth.

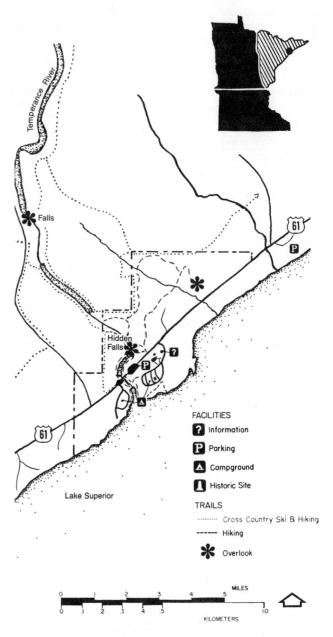

FACILITIES

?	Information
P	Parking
△	Campground
🏛	Historic Site

TRAILS

.... Cross Country Ski & Hiking

------- Hiking

✳ Overlook

This family is enjoying the view of the river gorge; typical of how rivers along the North Shore flow into Lake Superior.

Facilities & Activities

50 drive-in campsites
flush toilets (H)
vault toilets (H)
showers (H)
picnic area
fishing (lake & stream)
boat launch near park
winter access
8 miles of foot trails
8 miles of X-country ski trails

Tettegouche State Park

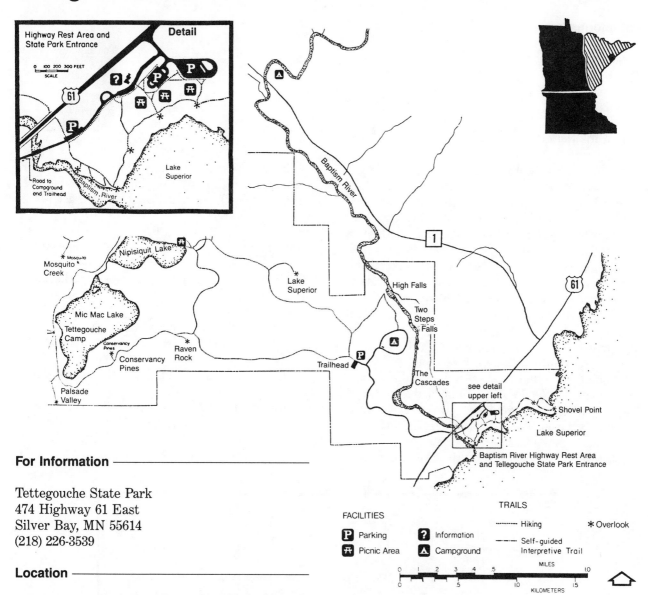

Detail

Highway Rest Area and State Park Entrance

0 100 200 300 FEET
SCALE

Road to Campground and Trailhead

Lake Superior

Baptism River

61

Baptism River

Mosquito Creek

Mosquito

Nipisiquit Lake

Lake Superior

Mic Mac Lake

Tettegouche Camp

Conservancy Pines

Conservancy Pines

Raven Rock

Trailhead

Palsade Valley

Baptism River

1

High Falls

Two Steps Falls

The Cascades

see detail upper left

61

Shovel Point

Lake Superior

Baptism River Highway Rest Area and Tellegouche State Park Entrance

FACILITIES

P Parking
ᛤ Picnic Area
? Information
▲ Campground

TRAILS

.... Hiking
— · — Self-guided Interpretive Trail
✱ Overlook

MILES
0 1 2 3 4 5   10
0   5   10   15
KILOMETERS

For Information

Tettegouche State Park
474 Highway 61 East
Silver Bay, MN 55614
(218) 226-3539

Location

Tettegouche State Park is located in Lake County, 4.5 miles northeast of Silver Bay on US 61. The 4,650-acre park contains a unique combination of natural features; rugged, semi-mountainous terrain, 1 mile of Lake Superior shoreline, 4 inland lakes, cascading rivers and waterfalls, and undisturbed northern hardwood forest. The best way to experience the complexity and diversity of Tettegouche's vegetative landscape is by hiking its trail system. High Falls, Minnesota's highest waterfall, is approximately a mile hike from the parking area near the Baptism River southwest of the visitor center. Shorter trails lead to numerous overlooks along the shoreline, including the precipitous cliffs of Shovel Point, the most prominent feature of the shoreline.

Facilities & Activities

34 drive-in campsites
flush toilets (H)
vault toilets (H)
winterized showers (H)
picnic area
fishing (stream, lake, & river)
visitor center (year-round)
winter access
14 miles of foot trails
2 miles of self-guided trails
11 miles of X-country ski trails
5 miles of snowmobile trails

Voyageurs National Park

For Information

Voyageurs National Park
P.O. Box 50
International Falls, MN 56649
(218) 283-9821

About the Park

Voyageurs National Park sits in the heart of Voyageur country and offers the visitor a kind of experience found nowhere else in the National Park system. Ancient rock exposures, outstanding lake country scenery, abundant wildlife, and over 200,000 acres with 30 lakes and 1600 islands distinguishes Voyageurs as a water-dominated park. Motorboat, houseboat, fishing boat, sailboat, canoe, kayak, and tour boat—these are the ways to experience Voyageurs National Park. The northern boundary of the park follows the U.S./Canadian border about 50 miles from east to west.

Voyageurs National Park is a vast and open space dominated by 4 major lakes (Kabetogama, Rainy, Namakan, and Sand Point) and myriad islands and bays. Boating in Voyageurs can be very rewarding, but it must be approached with caution. Storms can rise quickly and generate dangerous waves on the big lakes. Park Rangers patrol the large lakes daily and offer help and information to visitors. Ranger boats are identified by the National Park Service arrowhead on the boat hull and an American flag visible at the stern.

Park Access

Four major points provide access to the park along US 53 between Duluth and International Falls:

1. Traveling north, County Roads 23 and 24 from Orr lead to Crane Lake at the east end of the park.
2. County road 129 heads into Ash River and Kabetogama Narrows.
3. County Road 122 leads to Kabetogama Lake and the Kabetogama Lake Visitor Center.
4. State Highway 11, east from International Falls, provides access to the Island View area

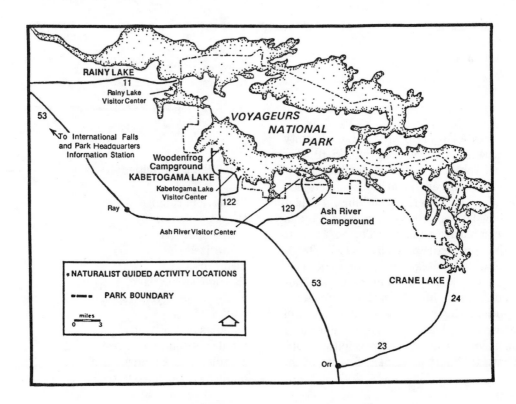

Park Rangers are available at the Visitor Centers to help you plan your trip to this water-dominated park.

and Rainy Lake Visitor Center on Rainy Lake at the northwest end of the park.

Camping in the Park

There are 120 designated individual campsites scattered throughout the park accessible only by boat or canoe. No permits or reservations are needed for camping. Each site provides for a tent pad, toilet, picnic table, fire ring with grate and are offered at no charge on a first-come, first-serve basis. Camping is not limited to these designated sites; there are approximately 400 additional traditionally used campsites with only a fire ring and a spot to pitch a tent. There is no restriction on group size, but most campsites have room for only 1 or possibly 2 tents. There are 2 designated group sites within the park. There are no restrictions on how camper's food is packaged, but campers are responsible for taking out their own garbage.

Camping Near the Park

Two state forest campgrounds offer limited services: Woodenfrog and Ash River. Woodenfrog Campground, northwest of Kabetogama Lake Visitor Center has 55 sites with water, vault toilets, and a swimming beach. Ash River Campground has 9 sites with water and vault toilets. Both campgrounds are open year-round.

A full range of automobile camping services are offered outside the park by private resorts in Rainy

Lake, Kabetogama Lake, Ash River, and Crane Lake. The park newspaper, the *Rendezvous*, gives a complete listing of these campgrounds and the services each provide.

Hiking

Voyageurs National Park has 32 miles of maintained hiking trails. All are accessible only by watercraft. If you don't have your own boat to get to the trailheads, you can rent one or use the taxi service many resort owners provide. No reservations or hiking permits are needed to use the park trails.

Winter Activities

In the winter, the 7-mile long Rainy Lake Ice Road provides auto access into the park. Snowmobiling in the park and surrounding areas offers miles of scenic trails. X-country skiing on groomed trails or through the backcountry can be an exhilarating experience. Snowshoeing and winter camping offer opportunities for the well-prepared and adventurous visitor. During freeze-up in late autumn and ice-out in early spring, the lakes are inaccessible.

Rainy Lake Visitor Center

Phone number: (218) 286-5258
Triple-wide public boat launch ramp
Courtesy day-use docking
Picnic area
Exhibit room
Park film
Interpretive literature sales
Ranger-guided activities
Tour boat service (49-passenger *The Pride of Rainy Lake*)

Kabetogama Lake Visitor Center

Phone number: (218) 875-2111
Double-wide public boat launch ramp
Courtesy day-use docking
Photographic exhibits
Park video tape
Interpretive literature sales
Ranger-guided activities
Tour boat service (17-passenger *Betsy Anna*)

Region 3

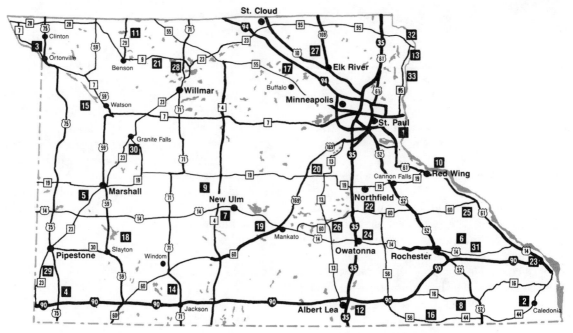

1—Afton State Park, 105
2—Beaver Creek Valley State Park, 106
3—Big Stone Lake State Park, 107
4—Blue Mounds State Park, 108
5—Camden State Park, 109
6—Carley State Park, 110
7—Flandrau State Park, 111
8—Forestville State Park, 112
9—Fort Ridgely State Park, 113
10—Frontenac State Park, 114
11—Glacial Lakes State Park, 115
12—Helmer Myre State Park, 116
13—Interstate State Park, 117–118
14—Kilen Woods State Park, 119
15—Lac Qui Parle State Park, 120
16—Lake Louise State Park, 121
17—Lake Maria State Park, 122

18—Lake Shetek State Park, 123
19—Minneopa State Park, 124
20—Minnesota Valley Trail State Park, 125
21—Monson Lake State Park, 126
22—Nerstrand Woods State Park, 127
23—O. L. Kipp State Park, 128
24—Rice Lake State Park, 129
25—Richard J. Dorer Memorial Hardwood State Forest, 130
26—Sakatah Lake State Park, 131
27—Sand Dunes State Forest, 132
28—Sibley State Park, 133
29—Split Rock Creek State Recreation Area, 134
30—Upper Sioux Agency State Park, 135
31—Whitewater State Park, 136–137
32—Wild River State Park, 138–139
33—William O'Brien State Park, 140

Afton State Park

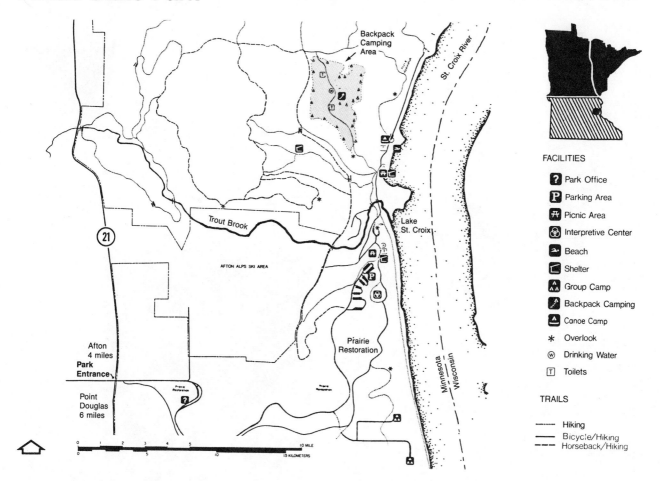

FACILITIES

- ? Park Office
- P Parking Area
- 🛆 Picnic Area
- 🌐 Interpretive Center
- 🏊 Beach
- ◤ Shelter
- 🏕 Group Camp
- 🏕 Backpack Camping
- 🛆 Canoe Camp
- * Overlook
- ⓦ Drinking Water
- ⊤ Toilets

TRAILS

- ········ Hiking
- ———— Bicycle/Hiking
- - - - - Horseback/Hiking

For Information

Afton State Park
6959 Peller Avenue South
Hastings, MN 55033
(612) 436-5391

Location

Afton State Park is located north of Hastings. Travel 3 miles east on US 10, then 7 miles north on County Road 21 to the junction of County Road 20. The 1,669-acre park lies on the bluffs overlooking the St. Croix River.

Facilities & Activities

24 backpack campsites
flush toilets (H)
vault toilets
2 rustic group camps
2 picnic areas (H)
enclosed & open shelters
swimming
fishing (river)
visitor center (year-round)
winter access
warming house
18 miles of foot trails
.5 mile of self-guided trails
5 miles of horseback riding trails
4 miles of bike trails
18 miles of X-country ski trails

About the Park

To preserve the natural character of the park, development has been kept to a minimum. The campground is a strenuous ¾-mile hike from the parking lots and the swimming beach and interior of the park are accessible only by trail. The park is cut by deep ravines that drop three hundred feet to the river. The rugged terrain offers challenging hiking and affords spectacular views of the St. Croix Valley.

Beaver Creek Valley State Park

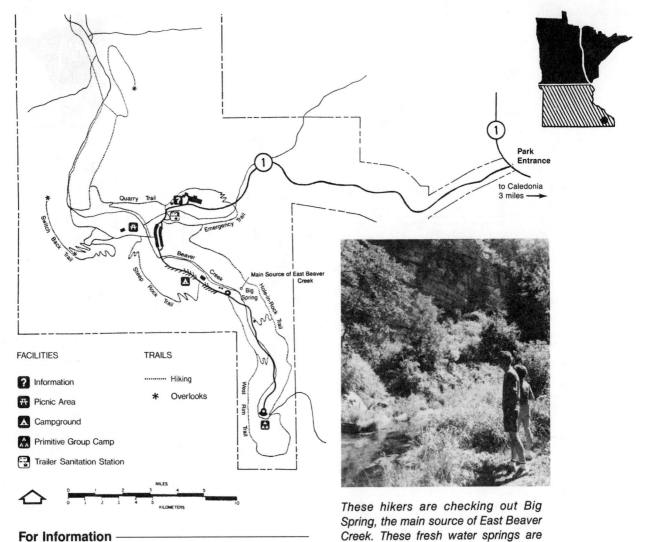

FACILITIES

?	Information
🛉	Picnic Area
⛺	Campground
⛺⛺	Primitive Group Camp
🚽	Trailer Sanitation Station

TRAILS

··········· Hiking

* Overlooks

These hikers are checking out Big Spring, the main source of East Beaver Creek. These fresh water springs are common along the valley walls in the vicinity of the park.

For Information

Beaver Creek Valley State Park
Rt. 2, Box 57
Caledonia, MN 55921
(507) 724-2107

Location

Beaver Creek Valley State Park, located in Houston County, is 5 miles west of Caledonia on County Road 1 off State Highway 76. The 1,214-acre park is situated in one of the most interesting geologic areas in Minnesota—the "driftless area." The area was untouched by most recent glacial advances; however, deep rugged valleys were carved as the glaciers receded. The valley walls of the park rise as much as 250 feet above spring-fed Beaver Creek, one of the best trout streams in southeastern Minnesota.

Facilities & Activities

42 drive-in campsites
6 walk-in campsites
16 campsites with electricity
dump station
vault toilets (H)
showers
rustic group camp (100 capacity)
picnic area with an enclosed shelter
fishing (stream)
visitor center (seasonal)
winter access
warming house
8 miles of foot trails
4 miles of X-country ski trails

Big Stone Lake State Park

For Information

Big Stone Lake State Park
Rt. 1, Box 153
Ortonville, MN 56278
(612) 839-3663

Location

Big Stone Lake State Park is split into two areas: Meadowbrook and Bonanza. The Meadowbrook area, the main campground, is approximately 7 miles northwest of Ortonville on State Highway 7. The Bonanza area, location of the primitive group camp and a day-use area, is an additional 12 miles to the northwest off of State Highway 7. The area around this 1,118-acre state park abounds with granite quarries and is rich in fossils and artifacts. Big Stone Lake is the source of the Minnesota River.

Facilities & Activities

42 drive-in campsites
10 campsites with electricity
dump station
vault toilets
rustic group camp
picnic area
swimming
fishing (lake)
boat launch
boat rental
winter access
1.5 miles of foot trails
3.5 miles of snowmobile trails

FACILITIES

? Information
Visitor Center
Picnic Area
Swimming Beach

Boat Ramp
Campground
Trailer Sanitation Station
Primitive Group Camp

TRAILS

········· Hiking

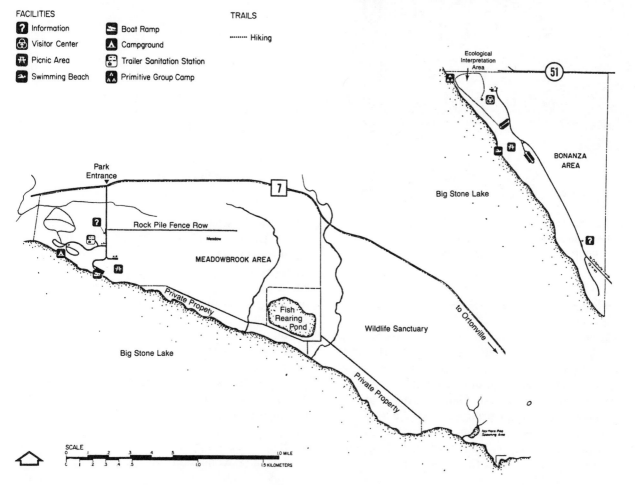

Blue Mounds State Park

For Information

Blue Mounds State Park
Rt. 1
Luverne, MN 56156
(507) 283-4892

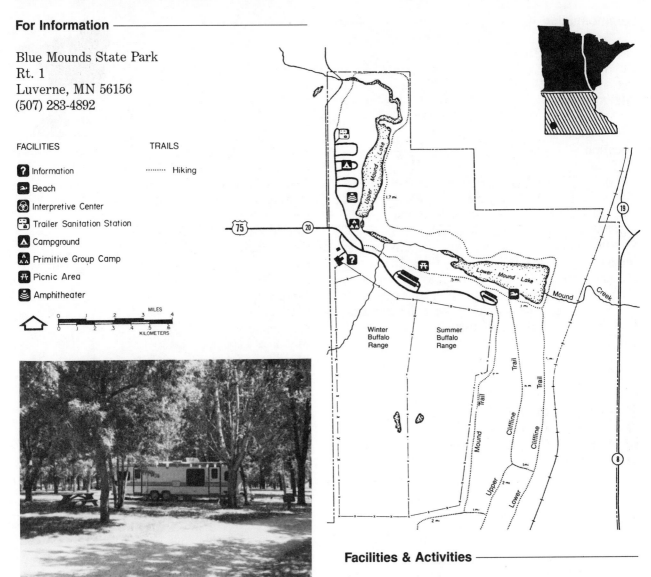

FACILITIES	TRAILS
? Information	.... Hiking
≥ Beach	
⊛ Interpretive Center	
⊞ Trailer Sanitation Station	
▲ Campground	
▲▲ Primitive Group Camp	
⊞ Picnic Area	
⊜ Amphitheater	

This motorhome is quite at home at Blue Mounds, one of the many state parks where facilities include electricity, pull-through sites, and a dump station.

Location

Blue Mounds State Park is located off of US 75 in Rock County, 6 miles north of Luverne and 16 miles south of Pipestone. The 1,500-acre park is one of the largest prairie parks in Minnesota and is the only state park where you will find buffalo (American Bison). Most of the park's prairie sits atop a massive outcrop of rock known as Sioux Quartzite. A cliff, 1½ miles long and at some points 90 feet high, provides a panoramic view of the countryside.

Facilities & Activities

73 drive-in campsites
40 campsites with electricity
dump station
flush toilets (H)
showers (H)
rustic group camp
picnic areas with open shelter
swimming
fishing (lake)
boat access (carry)
canoe rental
visitor center (seasonal)
interpretive program (seasonal)
winter access
13 miles of foot trails
3 miles of X-country ski trails
7 miles of snowmobile trails

Camden State Park

The swimming hole and beach at Camden State Park is one of the main attractions during the summer.

For Information

Camden State Park
Lynd, MN 56157
(507) 865-4530

Location

Camden State Park is located 8 miles southwest of Marshall off US 23 in Lyon County. The cool, wooded valley of Camden, called an oasis by pioneers, descends from the open prairie. The 1,666-acre park lies near the summit of a geological area that separates the Minnesota River and Missouri River watersheds.

Facilities & Activities

93 drive-in campsites
26 campsites with electricity
dump station
flush toilets (H)
vault toilets (H)
showers
rustic group camp (40 capacity)
2 picnic areas (H)
enclosed & open shelters
swimming
fishing (stream)
visitor center (seasonal)
interpretive program (seasonal)
winter access
warming house
skating rink
10 miles of foot trails
1 mile of self-guided trails
3.8 miles of bike riding trails
6 miles of X-country ski trails
8 miles of snowmobile trails

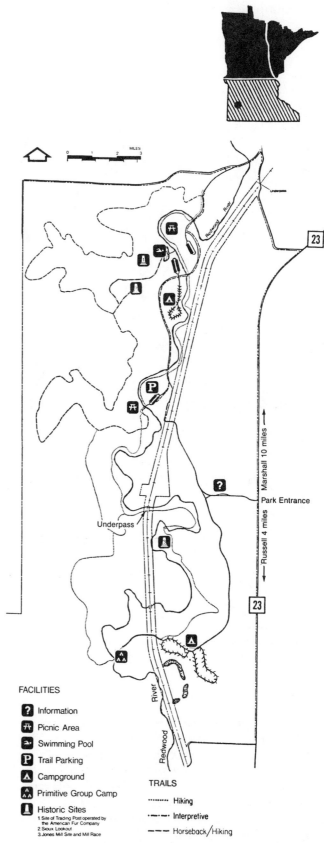

FACILITIES

? Information
Picnic Area
Swimming Pool
P Trail Parking
Campground
Primitive Group Camp
Historic Sites
1. Site of Trading Post operated by the American Fur Company
2. Sioux Lookout
3. Jones Mill Site and Mill Race

TRAILS

•••••• Hiking
•–•–• Interpretive
– – – Horseback/Hiking

REGION 3

Carley State Park

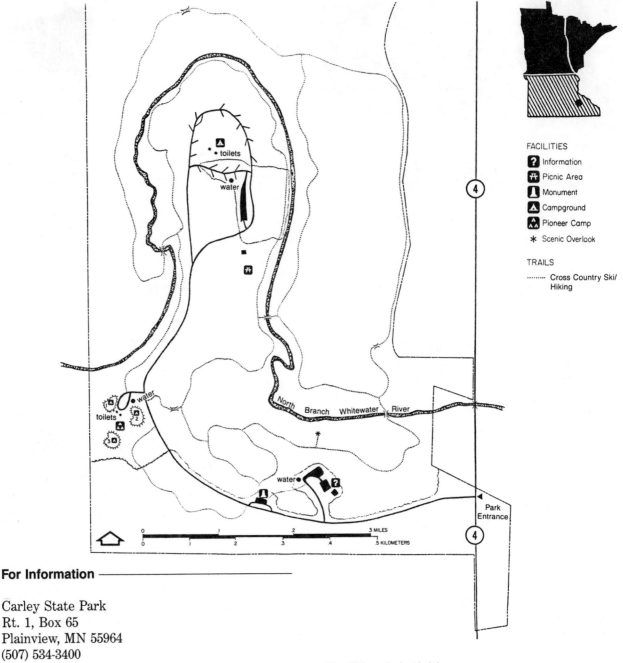

FACILITIES

? Information

🏕 Picnic Area

⚱ Monument

⛺ Campground

⛺ Pioneer Camp

✳ Scenic Overlook

TRAILS

········ Cross Country Ski/
Hiking

For Information

Carley State Park
Rt. 1, Box 65
Plainview, MN 55964
(507) 534-3400

Location

Carley State Park is located in Wabasha County, 4 miles south of Plainview on County Road 4. The 211-acre park is located in a transition zone between the hardwood forests of Minnesota's southeastern blufflands and its southern oak barrens. The north branch of the Whitewater River, a designated trout stream that runs through the park, provides good habitat for brown trout.

Facilities & Activities

20 drive-in campsites
vault toilets
3 rustic group camps (accommodates 25 each)
picnic areas
fishing (stream)
interpretive program (seasonal)
winter access
6 miles of foot trails
5 miles of X-country ski trails

Flandrau State Park

For Information

Flandrau State Park
1300 Summit Avenue
New Ulm, MN 56073
(507) 354-3519

Location

Flandrau State Park is adjacent to and partially within the city of New Ulm in Brown County. It is several blocks southwest of State Highways 15 and 68 and 2 miles south of US 14. The 805-acre park lies in a valley cut by the Cottonwood River, a scenic prairie river. Confining the river and forming the park's boundaries are steep slopes covered with cool, moist forests, and oak shaded bluffs.

Facilities & Activities

90 drive-in campsites
20 campsites with electricity
dump station
flush toilets (H)
vault toilets (H)
showers (H)
modern group camp (110 capacity)

rustic group camp (50 capacity)
picnic areas with enclosed shelter (H)
swimming pool with sand bottom & beachhouse
concession stand
fishing (river)
boat access (carry)
boat & canoe rental near park
visitor center (seasonal)
interpretive program (seasonal)
winter access
ski rental
8.5 miles of foot trails
1 mile of self-guided trail
7.5 miles X-country ski trails
1.3 miles of snowmobile trails

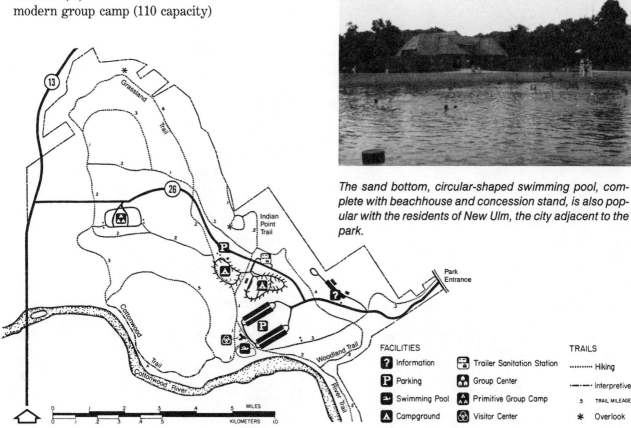

The sand bottom, circular-shaped swimming pool, complete with beachhouse and concession stand, is also popular with the residents of New Ulm, the city adjacent to the park.

FACILITIES

[?] Information
[P] Parking
[≈] Swimming Pool
[▲] Campground
[⊟] Trailer Sanitation Station
[♦♦] Group Center
[♦♦] Primitive Group Camp
[⊗] Visitor Center

TRAILS

.... Hiking
—·—·— Interpretive
.5 TRAIL MILEAGE
✳ Overlook

Park Entrance

Forestville State Park

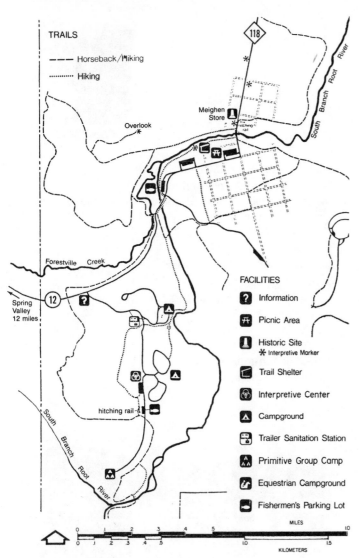

TRAILS

- – – – Horseback/Hiking
- ·········· Hiking

Overlook

Meighen Store

South Branch Root River

118

Forestville Creek

Spring Valley 12 miles

12

South Branch Root River

hitching rail

FACILITIES

- ? Information
- 🎪 Picnic Area
- 🏛 Historic Site
  ✳ Interpretive Marker
- Trail Shelter
- Interpretive Center
- ▲ Campground
- Trailer Sanitation Station
- Primitive Group Camp
- Equestrian Campground
- Fishermen's Parking Lot

MILES

KILOMETERS

For Information

Forestville State Park
Rt. 2, Box 128
Preston, MN 55965
(507) 352-5111

Location

Forestville State Park is located in Fillmore County about halfway between Spring Valley and Preston. The entrance to the park is located 4 miles south of US 16 on County Road 5, then 2 miles east on County Road 12. This 2,643-acre park is located in the "stream dissected" area of the state, where the landscape was sculpted by the erosive action of streams fed by glacial meltwater.

About the Park

Forestville State Park has the highest horseback use of any state park in Minnesota. The hilly terrain and winding streams provide interesting and scenic riding. The park has 3 clean, spring-fed streams with an abundance of brown, brook, and rainbow trout. There are many springs, underground rivers, caves, and sinkholes in the Forestville area. Mystery Cave, 5½ miles by road from the park, is managed as part of Forestville State Park. The cave is the largest natural cave in the state with 12 miles of natural caverns and passages. The cave remains a constant 47° year-round. Guided tours are offered every day between Memorial Day and Labor Day and last approximately one hour.

Facilities & Activities

73 drive-in campsites
23 campsites with electricity
dump station
flush toilets (H)
vault toilets (H)
showers (H)
horse camping (80 capacity)
rustic group camp (100 capacity)
picnic area (H)
enclosed & open shelters
fishing (stream)
visitor center (seasonal)
interpretive program (seasonal)
winter access
warming house
Meighen Store (19th century mercantile store, owned and operated by the Minnesota Historical Society)
15 miles of foot trails
14 miles of horseback riding trails
6.5 miles of X-country ski trails
9 miles of snowmobile trails

Fort Ridgely State Park

For Information

Fort Ridgely State Park
Rt. 1, Box 65
Fairfax, MN 55332
(507) 426-7840

Location

Fort Ridgely State Park is located 6 miles south of Fairfax along State Highway 4; the entrance is off Nicollet County Road 29. The park covers 504 acres of wooded ravines and open meadows on the north bluff of the Minnesota River Valley in Nicollet and Renville counties. The park is named after the military post that occupied the site in the 1850s and 1860s.

Facilities & Activities

39 drive-in campsites
4 backpack campsites
8 campsites with electricity
flush toilets
vault toilets
showers
horse camping
rustic group camp
picnic area (H)
enclosed & open shelters
visitor center (seasonal)
winter access
warming house
9-hole golf course
old fort site & interpretive center (operated by the Minnesota Historical Society)
10 miles of foot trails
7 miles of horseback riding trails
4.5 miles of X-country ski trails
7 miles of snowmobile trails

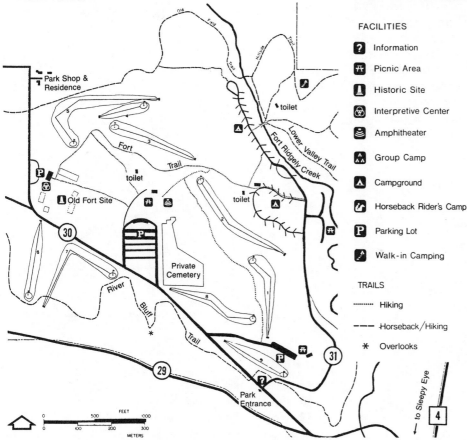

FACILITIES

? Information
Picnic Area
Historic Site
Interpretive Center
Amphitheater
Group Camp
Campground
Horseback Rider's Camp
P Parking Lot
Walk-in Camping

TRAILS

.... Hiking

--- Horseback/Hiking

* Overlooks

The memorial at the old fort site commemorates the participants of the Dakota conflict at Fort Ridgely.

REGION 3

Frontenac State Park

For Information

Frontenac State Park
Rt. 2, Box 134
Lake City, MN 55041
(612) 345-3401

Many hiking trails are designated as snowmobile trails in the winter; some are designated as cross-country ski trails.

Location

Frontenac State Park is located 10 miles southeast of Red Wing on Goodhue County Road 2, off of US 61. The 2,773-acre park is on the shore of Lake Pepin. Wooded bluffs high above the Mississippi River provide excellent vistas of the lake. Since 1900, Frontenac has been recognized as an excellent place to watch bird migration. Frontenac was in its heyday in the 1870s and '80s; today old Frontenac remains a nostalgic reminder of Minnesota's past.

Facilities & Activities

58 drive-in campsites
6 walk-in campsites
19 campsites with electricity
dump station
flush toilets (H)
showers (H)
rustic group camp (20 capacity)
picnic area (H)
enclosed shelter
fishing (lake & river)
boat launch near park
winter access
13 miles of foot trails
6 miles of X-country ski trails
8 miles of snowmobile trails

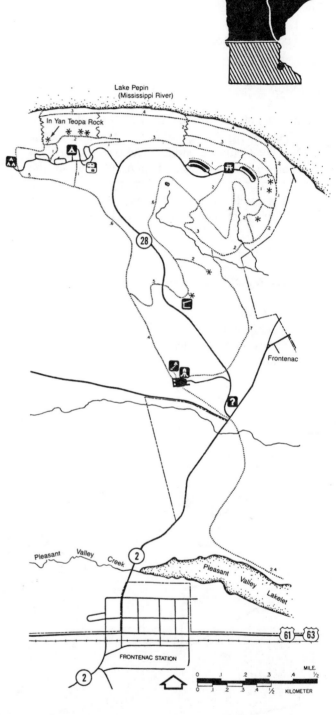

FACILITIES

? Information
Picnic Area
Trail Center
Trail Shelter

Campground
Primitive Group Camp
Backpack Campsites
Trailer Sanitation Station

TRAILS

Hiking
1.0 TRAIL DISTANCES IN MILES
* Overlooks

Glacial Lakes State Park

For Information

Glacial Lakes State Park
Rt. 2, Box 126
Starbuck, MN 56381
(612) 239-2860

Location

Glacial Lakes State Park is located 5 miles south of Starbuck off of State Highway 29. Entrance to the park is from Pope County Road 41. The 1,880-acre park is located in a geological area commonly known as the Leaf Hills—a band of glacial hills unlike any other in the state. At Glacial Lakes you can see many typical glacial landscape features such as kames, kettles, eskers, and moraines—geologists' terms for specific landscape formations.

Facilities & Activities

39 drive-in campsites
2 backpack campsites
14 campsites with electricity
dump station

flush toilets (H)
vault toilets (H)
showers (H)
horse camping
rustic group camp
picnic areas with open shelter
swimming
fishing (lake)
boat launch
boat & canoe rental
boat motor restrictions
winter access
14 miles of foot trails
.6 mile of self-guided trails
7 miles of horseback riding trails
5 miles of X-country ski trails
11 miles of snowmobile trails

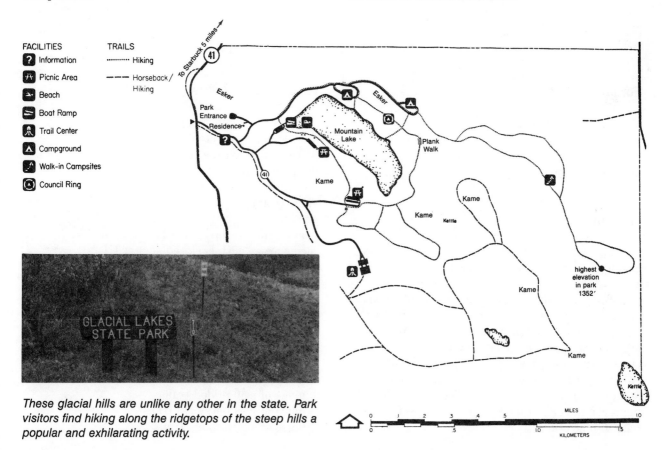

These glacial hills are unlike any other in the state. Park visitors find hiking along the ridgetops of the steep hills a popular and exhilarating activity.

REGION 3

Helmer Myre State Park

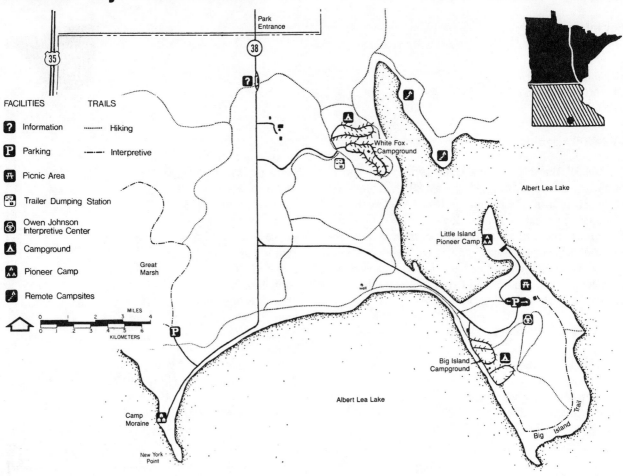

FACILITIES

- ❓ Information
- 🅿 Parking
- 🏕 Picnic Area
- Trailer Dumping Station
- Owen Johnson Interpretive Center
- 🅰 Campground
- Pioneer Camp
- Remote Campsites

TRAILS

- .... Hiking
- ·—·—· Interpretive

MILES

KILOMETERS

Park Entrance

White Fox Campground

Albert Lea Lake

Little Island Pioneer Camp

Great Marsh

Big Island Campground

Albert Lea Lake

Camp Moraine

New York Point

Big Island Trail

For Information

Helmer Myre State Park
Rt. 3, Box 33
Albert Lea, MN 56007
(507) 373-5084

Location

Helmer Myre State Park is located in Freeborn County 3 miles southeast of Albert Lea, on County Road 38. Exit 11 on I-35 is the most convenient approach to the park. The rolling hills, shallow lakes, and marshes of this 1,587-acre park were formed as the last major glacier retreated from Minnesota 10,000 years ago. The glacial features found here include moraines, a moraine dam lake, and an esker. Albert Lea Lake has a surface area of 2,600 acres and over 70 miles of shoreline. Pelicans are becoming a common sight on Albert Lea, especially during fall migration.

Facilities & Activities

100 drive-in campsites in 2 campgrounds
4 backpack campsites
31 campsites with electricity
dump station
flush toilets (H)
showers (H)
semi-modern group camp (New York Point)
rustic group camp (Little Island Pioneer)
picnic areas with enclosed shelter (H)
fishing (lake)
boat launch
canoe rental
visitor center (year-round)
interpretive program (year-round)
winter access
warming house
16 miles of foot trails
3 miles of self-guided trails
8 miles of X-country ski trails
7 miles of snowmobile trails

Interstate State Park

A scenic overlook provides a breathtaking view of the scenic river gorge, the St. Croix Dalles. A favorite activity at the park is to paddle from the campground canoe rental concession upstream to view the Dalles; then head downstream for a 7-mile trip to the National Park Service Osceola Canoe Landing . . . or the 17-mile trip to William O'Brien State Park.

For Information

Interstate State Park
Box 254
Taylors Falls, MN 55084
(612) 465-5711

Location

Interstate State Park is on the southern edge of the city of Taylors Falls on the St. Croix River. The park entrance is on State Highway 95/US 8. In Chisago County, this 293-acre park was established in 1895, making it the second park in the Minnesota state park system.

About the Park

Interstate is the first park in the nation created as part of a cooperative venture between 2 states. Wisconsin's Interstate Park is the "other half" of this venture. In 1968, the U.S. Congress designated the St. Croix as a Wild and Scenic River, the first in the nation. The main feature of Interstate State Park is the scenic river gorge, the St. Croix Dalles, with its high cliffs and world-famous glacial potholes. The park contains more potholes in a smaller area than any other other location in the world, and has the world's deepest potholes as well. The deepest one that has been measured accurately, the "Bottomless Pit," is over 60 feet deep and 12–15 feet wide. The St. Croix Dalles can also be enjoyed from aboard authentic sternwheel riverboats that dock at the park's northern end in Taylors Falls. Kayaking, canoeing, and rock climbing are popular activities of park visitors.

Facilities & Activities

48 drive-in campsites
24 campsites with electricity
dump station
flush toilets (H)
vault toilets (H)
showers (H)
rustic group camp (200 capacity)
picnic areas with 2 shelters (1 enclosed, 1 open)
fishing (river)
boat launch
canoe rental
visitor center (seasonal)
interpretive program (seasonal)
winter access
canoe shuttle
museum
3 miles of foot trails

Interstate State Park (continued)

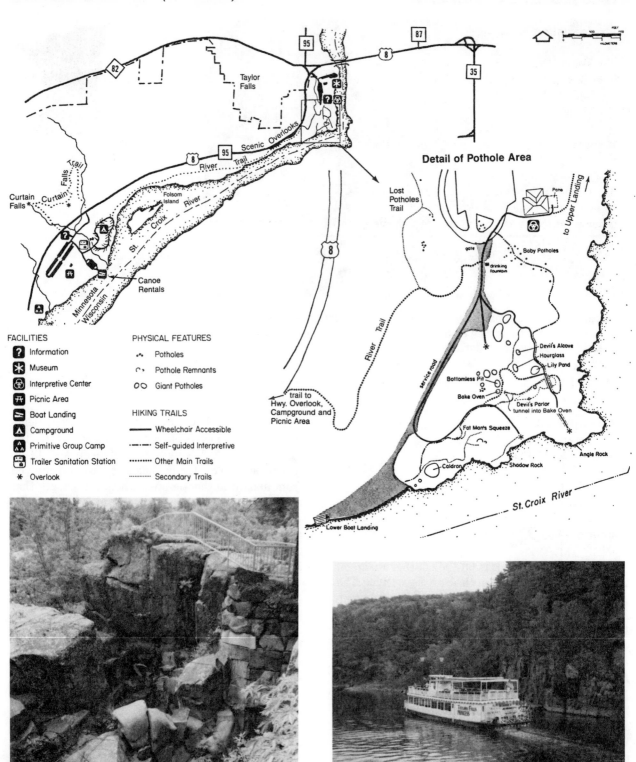

FACILITIES

- **?** Information
- **✳** Museum
- **⊕** Interpretive Center
- **⊼** Picnic Area
- **⇌** Boat Landing
- **⛺** Campground
- **⋀** Primitive Group Camp
- **⬚** Trailer Sanitation Station
- **✳** Overlook

PHYSICAL FEATURES

- Potholes
- Pothole Remnants
- Giant Potholes

HIKING TRAILS

- ──── Wheelchair Accessible
- ─·─·─ Self-guided Interpretive
- ········ Other Main Trails
- ·········· Secondary Trails

Detail of Pothole Area

Geologists come from all over the world to study these intriguing rock formations; rock climbers come for a different reason!

Authenic sternwheel riverboats tour the St. Croix Dalles; tourists may board at the docks in Taylor Falls, at the park's northern end.

Kilen Woods State Park

For Information

Kilen Woods State Park
Rt. 1, Box 122
Lakefield, MN 56150-9566
(507) 662-6258

Location

Kilen Woods State Park is located 9 miles northeast of Lakefield in Jackson County. The park entrance is on County Road 24, 5 miles east of State Highway 86. Nestled in the wooded hillsides and grassy ravines along the west bank of the Des Moines River, these 200 acres of nature and tranquility have been referred to as "an oasis in the farm belt" of Minnesota.

Facilities & Activities

33 drive-in campsites
4 walk-in campsites
3 canoe campsites
11 campsites with electricity
dump station
vault toilets (H)
showers (H)
rustic group camp
picnic area
multipurpose year-round shelter
fishing (river)
boat access (carry)
boat & canoe rental near park
visitor center (seasonal)
interpretive program (seasonal)
winter access
warming house
ski rental
skating rink
lookout tower
5 miles of foot trails
1.5 miles of X-country ski trails
3.5 miles of snowmobile trails

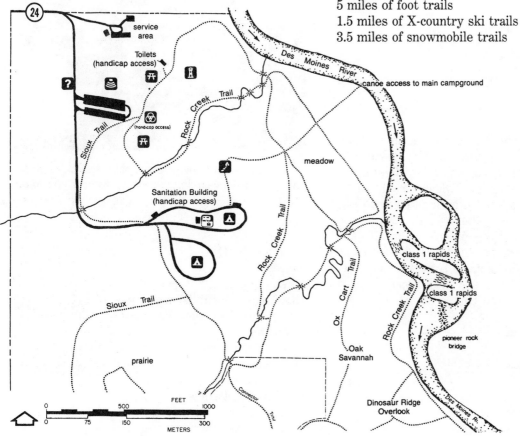

FACILITIES

?   Information

⛫   Picnic Area

🏕   Campground

Walk-in Camping

Trailer Dump Station

Interpretive / Trail Center (Picnic Shelter)

Lookout Tower

Amphitheater

TRAILS

·········   Hiking

REGION 3

Lac Qui Parle State Park

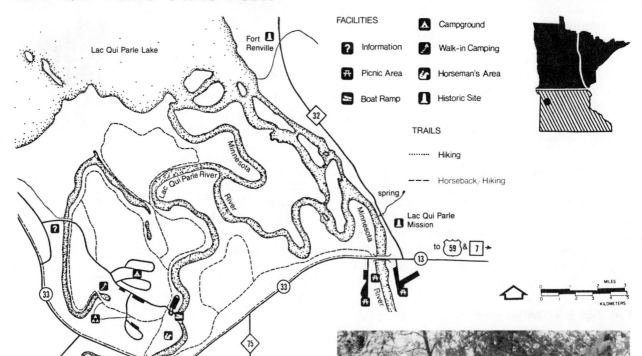

FACILITIES

- 🅰 Campground
- ❓ Information
- ⛷ Walk-in Camping
- 🅰 Picnic Area
- 🐎 Horseman's Area
- 🚣 Boat Ramp
- 🏛 Historic Site

TRAILS

········ Hiking

- - - - Horseback / Hiking

For Information

Lac Qui Parle State Park
Rt. 5, Box 74A
Montevideo, MN 56265
(612) 752-4736

Location

Lac Qui Parle State Park is located in Lac Qui Parle County, 12 miles northwest of Montevideo on the Minnesota River. Access is by Chippewa County Road 13 and Lac Qui Parle County Road 33. The 530-acre park is the southern gateway to Lac Qui Parle Lake, a broadening of the Minnesota River in the Glacial River Warren valley. To the north and west of the park is the 27,000-acre Lac Qui Parle Wildlife Management Area, which has become one of the biggest and most popular goose management areas in the United States.

Facilities & Activities

50 drive-in campsites
6 walk-in campsites
5 backpack campsites
22 campsites with electricity
dump station

Bird watchers would love this campsite; they could probably view the early morning songsters without getting out of bed!

flush toilets (H)
showers (H)
horse camping (100 capacity)
rustic group camp (50 capacity)
picnic area with open shelter (H)
swimming
fishing (lake & river)
boat launch
winter access
6 miles of foot trails
6 miles of horseback riding trails
6 miles of X-country ski trails

Lake Louise State Park

For Information

Lake Louise State Park
Rt. 1, Box 184
Le Roy, MN 55951
(507) 324-5249

Location

Lake Louise State Park is located in Mower County, 1½ miles north of LeRoy on County Road 14 north of State Highway 56. The 1,168-acre park contains 2 spring-fed streams that join in the park to form the Iowa River, a dam, and impoundment where a grist mill was located in the late 1800s. Many species of wildlife are attracted by the diverse habitat of hardwood forest and old field areas found in the park.

Facilities & Activities

22 drive-in campsites
11 campsites with electricity
dump station
vault toilets (H)
showers
horse camping (50 capacity)
rustic group camp (100 capacity)
picnic areas with open shelter (H)
swimming
fishing (lake & stream)
boat access (carry)
Hambrecht Historical Cottage & Museum
  (seasonal)
winter access
boat motor restrictions
11 miles of foot trails
1.2 miles of self-guided trails
7 miles of horseback riding trails
4 miles of X-country ski trails
7 miles of snowmobile trails

An open shelter like this one at Lake Louise is a great place for a family reunion or a group picnic; nearly three-fourths of the state parks have picnic areas with shelters—some open, some enclosed.

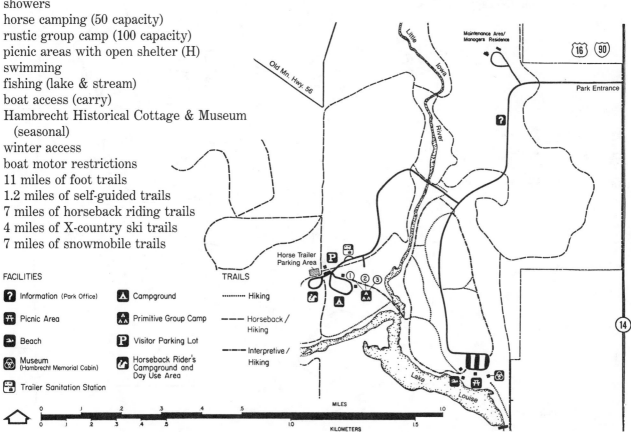

FACILITIES

? Information (Park Office)	**A** Campground
⚷ Picnic Area	**A** Primitive Group Camp
⚊ Beach	**P** Visitor Parking Lot
⚙ Museum (Hambrecht Memorial Cabin)	**⚞** Horseback Rider's Campground and Day Use Area
⚏ Trailer Sanitation Station	

TRAILS

.... Hiking

— — — Horseback / Hiking

—·—·— Interpretive / Hiking

Lake Maria State Park

For Information

Lake Maria State Park
Rt. 1, Box 128
Monticello, MN 55362
(612) 878-2325

Location

Lake Maria State Park is located in Wright County, 8 miles west of I-94 at Monticello via County Road 39, then right on County Road 111 to the park entrance. The 1,418-acre park is located at the northern end of the Big Woods Moraine region and is a meld of rough and rolling hills. This kind of topography is typical of landscapes formed by re-treating glaciers. There are no drive-in campsites at Lake Maria (pronounced "Mariah") State park—only walk-in sites for backpackers.

fishing (lake)
boat launch
boat & canoe rental
visitor center (year-round)
winter access
warming house
skating rink
14 miles of foot trails
7 miles of horse trails
14 miles of X-country ski trails

Facilities & Activities

11 backpack campsites
vault toilets (H)
rustic group camp (50 capacity)
picnic area (H)

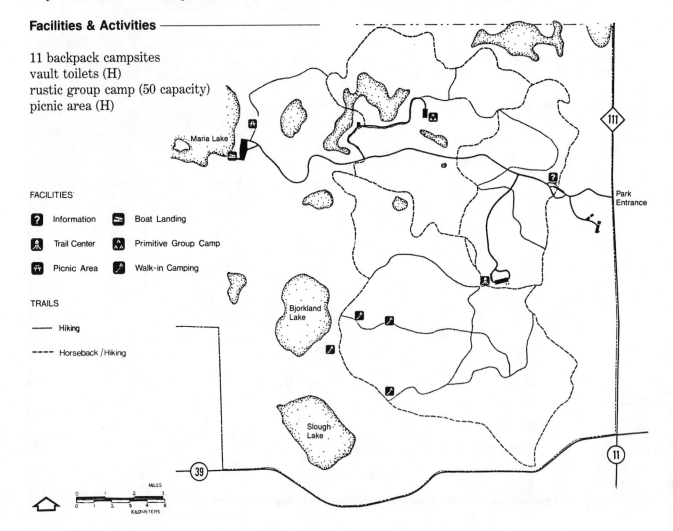

FACILITIES

❓ Information
🏕 Trail Center
🌲 Picnic Area

🛶 Boat Landing
⛺ Primitive Group Camp
🏕 Walk-in Camping

TRAILS

······ Hiking

- - - - Horseback / Hiking

Lake Shetek State Park

For Information

Lake Shetek State Park
Rt. 1, Box 164
Currie, MN 56123
(507) 763-3256

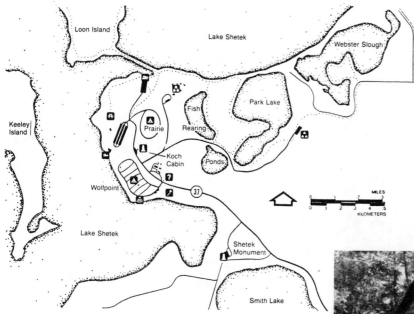

FACILITIES

? Information	▲ Campground
♣ Picnic Area	⚑ Walk-in Camping
⚊ Beach	⚐ Group Camp
⚓ Boat Ramp	⚐ Primitive Group Camp
⚑ Historic Site	⬥ Amphitheater

TRAILS

········ Hiking

Location

Lake Shetek State Park is located 14 miles northeast of Slayton in Murray County. Access to the park is by County Road 38, north of Currie at State Highway 30. Lake Shetek, the largest lake in southwestern Minnesota, forms the headwaters basin for the Des Moines River. Bird watching is a major activity at this 1,175-acre park. Loon Island, connected to the mainland by a causeway, is a bird sanctuary.

The Koch cabin, one of two historic sites at the park, is a remnant of the pioneer days.

Facilities & Activities

98 drive-in campsites
10 walk-in campsites
67 campsites with electricity
dump station
flush toilets (H)
vault toilets (H)
showers (H)
modern group camp (80 capacity)
rustic group camp (50 capacity)
picnic areas (1 open shelter; 1 enclosed shelter)
swimming

fishing (lake)
boat & canoe launch
boat & canoe rental
visitor center (seasonal)
interpretive program (seasonal)
winter access
snacks
2 historic sites—Koch cabin & Shetek Monument
5.5 miles of foot trails
1.5 miles of X-country ski trails
4.5 miles of snowmobile trails

REGION 3

Minneopa State Park

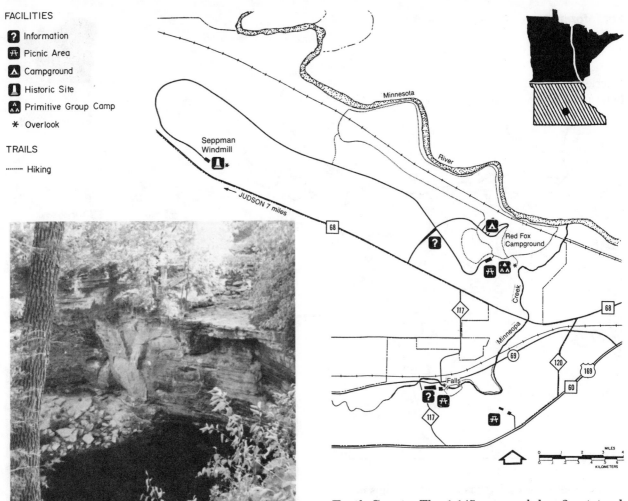

FACILITIES

- **?** Information
- **⊼** Picnic Area
- **△** Campground
- **⌷** Historic Site
- **⋀⋀** Primitive Group Camp
- ***** Overlook

TRAILS

------ Hiking

Seppman Windmill

JUDSON 7 miles

Minnesota River

Red Fox Campground

Creek

Minneopa

Falls

Park visitors are quite disappointed when, because of drought, the double waterfalls are absent. However, the deep gorge below the falls still provides an awesome sight.

For Information

Minneopa State Park
Rt. 9, Box 143
Mankato, MN 56001
(507) 625-4388

Location

Minneopa State Park is located off US 169 and State Highway 68, 5 miles west of Mankato in Blue Earth County. The 1,145-acre park has 2 outstanding geological features: the double waterfalls and the giant boulders on the park's grassland areas. The word Minneopa means "water falling twice" in the Dakota Indian language. The water from Minneopa Creek drops 45 feet into the deep gorge below the falls.

Facilities & Activities

62 drive-in campsites
flush toilets (H)
vault toilets (H)
showers (H)
rustic group camp (50 capacity)
3 picnic areas
2 open shelters (100 capacity)
fishing (stream)
winter access
historic site—Seppmann windmill
5 miles of foot trails
4 miles of X-country ski trails

Minnesota Valley Trail State Park

For Information

Minnesota Valley Trail Manager
19825 Park Blvd.
Jordan, MN 55352
(612) 492-6400

About the Trail

The Minnesota Valley Trail State Park was established by the state legislature in 1969 to provide a recreational travel route through the lower Minnesota River Valley, between Fort Snelling and Le Sueur. Eventually, 24,000 acres of floodplain marsh, grassland, and woodland will be included within state park, state trail, and the Minnesota Valley National Wildlife Refuge lands. When completed, nearly 75 miles of trails will traverse parts of Hennepin, Dakota, Scott, Carver, Sibley, and Le Sueur Counties. The trails will follow the Minnesota River from Fort Snelling State Park to the City of Le Sueur. *As of 1989, only the portion of the trail system from Belle Plaine to Chaska and Shakopee is completed.*

The state trail is managed by the Minnesota Department of Natural Resources, Division of Parks and Recreation. Upon completion, this state trail will be a multi-use recreational corridor through the entire lower Minnesota River Valley. It will link with other metro area trails and provide hiking, bicycling, horseback riding, snowmobiling, and X-country skiing opportunities.

Location

The Lawrence Unit (Headquarters) is located between Jordan and Belle Plaine on County Road 57, which is just north of US 169. Since the Lawrence Unit is the only unit where family and group camping have been developed, information is included here. For information on facilities at other com-

pleted units of the trail, contact the Minnesota Valley Trail Manager.

Facilities & Activities

25 walk-in campsites
8 walk-in campsites
1 canoe campsite
1 walk-in canoe campsite (by Paine Pond)
vault toilets (H)
horse camping
rustic group camp
picnic area for group use (H)
trail center
fishing (lake & river)
boat launch (near park)
winter access
warming house
historic site
4-mile loop for hiking
trail access to 22 miles of multi-use trails

TRAILS
········· Hiking
--- Horseback/Hiking/Mountain Bike

Scale in Miles

FACILITIES

? Information (Park Office)

🏕 Picnic Area

🧍 Trail Center

🏛 Historic Site

⛵ Canoe Campsite

⛺ Campground

⛺⛺ Primitive Group Camp

🚶 Walk-in Campsites

Monson Lake State Park

For Information

Monson Lake State Park
Sunburg, MN 56289
(612) 366-3797

Location

Monson Lake State Park is located 4 miles southwest of Sunburg in Swift County. Access is off State Highway 104, via County Road 18, just south of Sunburg. Small and quiet, the park consists of 187 acres of Monson and West Sunburg Lakes. The variety of birds in the park is spectacular—pelicans, a variety of herons, western grebes, shorebirds, and waterfowl.

Facilities & Activities

20 drive-in campsites
vault toilets
picnic area with open shelter
fishing (lake)
boat launch
1 mile of foot trails

This park features quiet and solitude, as well as excellent fishing, semi-primitive camping, canoeing, and birdwatching.

FACILITIES

? Information
🏕 Picnic Area
🪧 Historic Site
🚤 Boat Ramp
⛺ Campground

TRAILS

········ Hiking

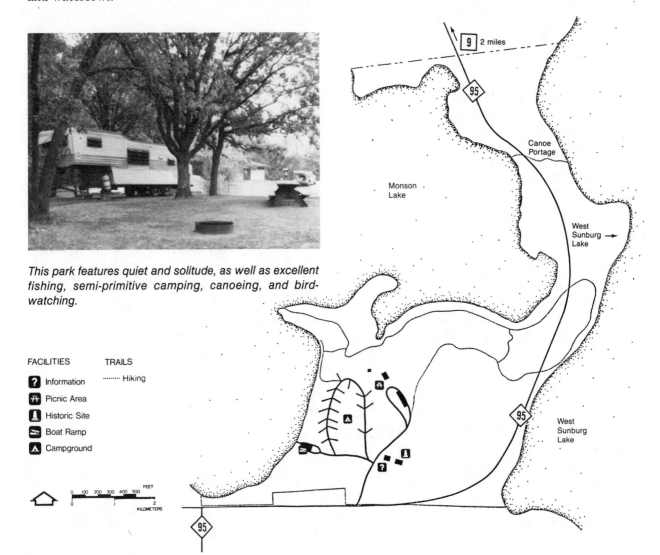

Nerstrand Woods State Park

For Information

Nerstrand Woods State Park
9700 170th St. East
Nerstrand, MN 55053·
(507) 334-8848

Location

Nerstrand Woods State Park is located in the eastern part of Rice County. From the north, the park is approximately 11 miles southeast of Northfield; from State Highway 3, take State Highway 246 southeast out of Northfield and follow signs to Nerstrand. From the south, the park is 12 miles northeast of Fairbault; take County Road 20 northeast from State Highway 60 East out of Fairbault, turn right on County Road 27 at Cannon City to Nerstrand, follow sign to park. This 1,280-acre park comprises one of the last remnants of the Big Woods along with its rolling hills and valleys traversed by Prairie Creek with its picturesque waterfalls.

Facilities & Activities

78 drive-in campsites
23 campsites with electricity
dump station
flush toilets (H)
vault toilets (H)
showers (H)
rustic group camp (200 capacity)
picnic area with open shelter
winter access
13 miles of foot trails
8 miles of X-country ski trails
5 miles of snowmobile trails

Nerstrand Woods, a good example of a forested recreation area, was established to preserve the nature and aesthetic features of the Big Woods; 13 miles of hiking trails makes the area quite accessible.

FACILITIES
- ? Information
- 🖾 Picnic Area
- 🅰 Campground
- Pioneer Camp
- Trailer Sanitation Station

TRAILS
- ---- Hiking

White Oak Trail .9 mi.
.1 mi.
Hidden Falls
Beaver Trail
Oak Bridge
.5 mi.
Prairie Creek
.1 mi.
.1 mi.
.2 mi.
.2 mi.
.1 mi.
.2 mi.
.1 mi.
.2 mi.
.1 mi.
Beaver Trail
.2 mi.
.5 mi.
88
← to FARIBAULT 10 miles
Basswood Trail
.3 mi.
Ranger Residence
to NERSTRAND → 2 miles
40
Fox Trail .5 mi.

SCALE
MILES
0 .1 .2 .25
0 1 2 3 4
KILOMETERS

REGION 3

O.L. Kipp State Park

For Information

O.L. Kipp State Park
Rt. 4
Winona, MN 55987
(507) 643-6849

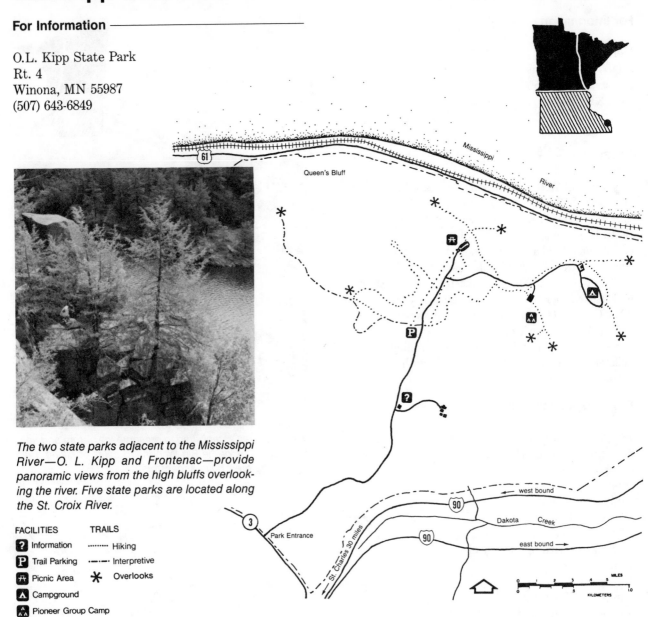

The two state parks adjacent to the Mississippi River—O. L. Kipp and Frontenac—provide panoramic views from the high bluffs overlooking the river. Five state parks are located along the St. Croix River.

FACILITIES		TRAILS	
?	Information	....	Hiking
P	Trail Parking	—·—·—	Interpretive
🏕	Picnic Area	✳	Overlooks
▲	Campground		
⛺	Pioneer Group Camp		

Location

O.L. Kipp State Park is located in Winona County about 20 miles southeast of Winona at the Junction of US 61 and I-90. Entrance to the park is off I-90 at the County Road 12 exit. On the north side of I-90 take County Road 3 (Apple Blossom Drive) to the park entrance. The creation of this park in 1976 on a bluff overlooking the Mississippi River Valley grew from a need for better access to the bluffland area of southeastern Minnesota. This park's 2,835 acres lie within the Richard J. Dorer Memorial Hardwood Forest. Classified as a "Natural State Park," the park emphasizes protection, perpetuation, and restoration of natural resources.

Facilities & Activities

31 drive-in campsites
vault toilets
rustic group camp
picnic area
winter access
6.5 miles of foot trails
1 mile of self-guided trails
9 miles of X-country ski trails

Rice Lake State Park

For Information

Rice Lake State Park
Route 1
Owatonna, MN 55060
(507) 451-7406

Location

Rice Lake State Park is located 7 miles east of Owatonna on Steele County Road 19. Rice Lake is a headwater source for the Zumbro River; its outlet forming the South Branch of the Middle Fork. This 1,060-acre park is very attractive to waterfowl because of the lake's shallow nature and marshy edges. It is the only lake of any size for many miles that water-oriented migrating birds can use to stop, rest, and feed. Rice Lake is named for the wild rice that Indians gathered here.

Even senior citizens enjoy the playground . . . particularly, when they think no one is watching!

Facilities & Activities

42 drive-in campsites
5 canoe campsites
16 campsites with electricity
dump station
flush toilets (H)
vault toilets (H)
showers (H)
rustic group camp (100 + capacity)
picnic area with open shelter
swimming
fishing (lake)
boat launch
canoe rental
visitor center (seasonal)
winter access
3 miles of foot trails
3.5 miles of X-country ski trails
1.5 miles of snowmobile trails

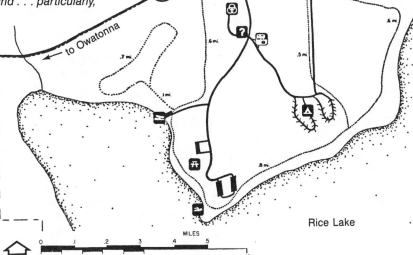

FACILITIES   TRAILS

?	Information	········· Hiking
卉	Picnic Area	
⮆	Beach	
⮱	Boat Landing	
⊛	Interpretive Center	
▲	Campground	
⚏	Primitive Group Camp	
⬟	Canoe Campground	
⊞	Trailer Sanitation Station	

Richard J. Dorer Memorial Hardwood State Forest

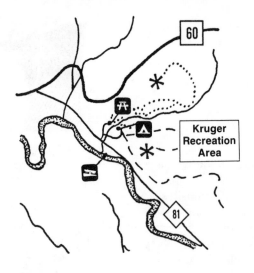

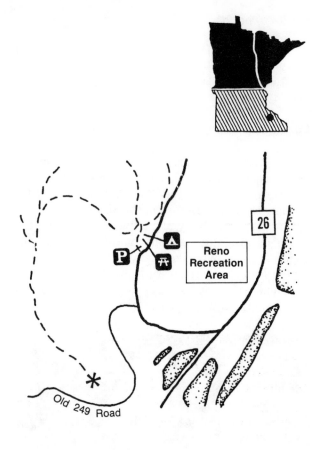

About the Forest

Of the 56 state forests in Minnesota, the Richard J. Dorer Memorial Hardwood State Forest is the largest. It covers parts of 8 counties and contains about 38,000 acres of state forest land for public use. There are recreation areas on 9 of the management units, with numerous miles of hiking, horseback, X-country ski, and snowmobile trails. Three of the units allow camping: Kruger, Reno, and Zumbro Bottoms. Zumbro Bottoms, located southwest of Kruger on the Zumbro River has an extensive trail system for horse traffic. Camping is permitted at the north, west, and main assembly areas.

Kruger Recreation Area

For Information

Area Forest Supervisor
Box 69
Lake City, MN 55041
(612) 345-3216

Location

On steep slopes overlooking the Zumbro River. From Wabasha, take CR 60 west for 5 miles, then CR 81 for .5 mile. Can also be reached by taking CR 81 from Kellogg.

Facilities & Activities

19 campsites
fee area
drinking water
13 picnic sites
water access
fishing
3 marked trails

Reno Recreation Area

For Information

Area Forest Supervisor
Box 278
Lewiston, MN 55952
(507) 523-2183

Location

Located on the bluffs overlooking the Mississippi River, .5 mile north of Reno off of SH 26.

Facilities

5 campsites
drinking water
9.5 miles of multiple use trails

Sakatah Lake State Park

For Information

Sakatah Lake State Park
Rt. 2, Box 19
Waterville, MN 56096
(507) 362-4438

Location

Sakatah Lake State Park is located on the border of Le Sueur and Rice Counties, 14 miles west of Fairbault. The park entrance is off of State Highway 60, 1 mile east of Waterville. The 842-acre parklands include 3.5 miles of shoreland along Sakatah Lake, a natural widening of the Cannon River. The Indians named this area Sakatah, which translates to "Singing Hills," hence the name for the state trail that runs through the park. The 42-mile multiple use trail, developed on an abandoned railroad grade, provides a limestone hard surface treadway for bicyclists, hikers, skiers, and snowmobilers.

Wait for me . . . I know it's time to go, but I wanted to hike just one more trail!

Facilities & Activities

63 drive-in campsites
14 campsites with electricity
dump station
flush toilets (H)
showers (H)
rustic group camp
picnic area
swimming
fishing (lake)
boat launch
canoe rental
visitor center (seasonal)
interpretive program (seasonal)
winter access
5 miles of foot trails
2 miles of X-country ski trails
access to 40 miles of hiking, biking, skiing, and snowmobile trails on the Sakatah Singing Hills State Trail

FACILITIES

?	Information	🚻	Trailer Sanition Station
🧺	Picnic Area	▲	Campground
👁	Visitor Center		TRAILS
🏖	Beach	....	Hiking
🚤	Water Access	— — —	State Trail (Multiple-use)

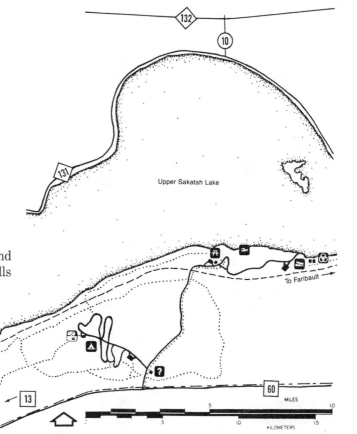

Sand Dunes State Forest

(Ann Lake Campground)

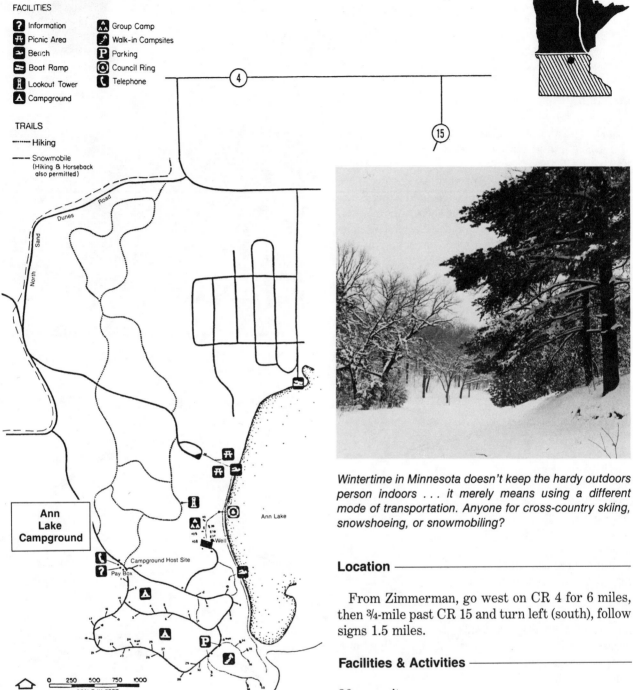

FACILITIES

? Information
🏕 Picnic Area
🏊 Beach
🚤 Boat Ramp
🔭 Lookout Tower
⛺ Campground

🏕 Group Camp
🚶 Walk-in Campsites
P Parking
Ⓒ Council Ring
📞 Telephone

TRAILS

···· Hiking
— — Snowmobile
(Hiking & Horseback
also permitted)

Ann
Lake
Campground

Campground Host Site

Pay Box

Well

Ann Lake

0 250 500 750 1000
SCALE IN FEET

Wintertime in Minnesota doesn't keep the hardy outdoors person indoors ... it merely means using a different mode of transportation. Anyone for cross-country skiing, snowshoeing, or snowmobiling?

Location

From Zimmerman, go west on CR 4 for 6 miles, then ¾-mile past CR 15 and turn left (south), follow signs 1.5 miles.

Facilities & Activities

36 campsites
fee area
drinking water
7 picnic sites
swimming
fishing
group camping
2-mile hiking trail

For Information

Area Forest Supervisor
915 South Highway #65
Cambridge, MN 55008
(612) 689-2832

Sibley State Park

For Information

Sibley State Park
800 Sibley Park Road N.E.
New London, MN 56273
(612) 354-2055

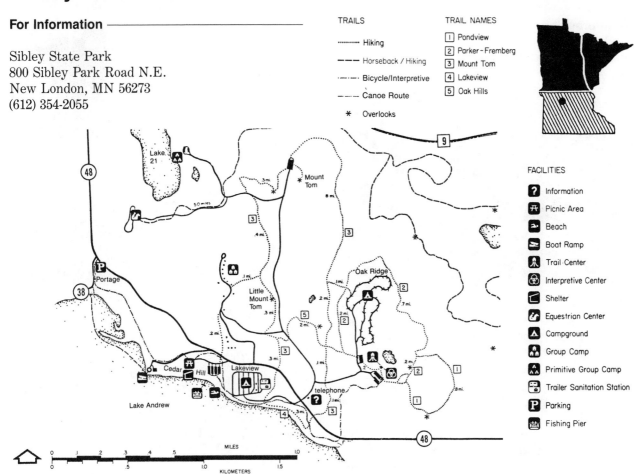

TRAILS
- ·········· Hiking
- — — Horseback / Hiking
- —·—·— Bicycle/Interpretive
- — — — Canoe Route
- * Overlooks

TRAIL NAMES
1. Pondview
2. Parker – Fremberg
3. Mount Tom
4. Lakeview
5. Oak Hills

FACILITIES
- ? Information
- 🛆 Picnic Area
- Beach
- Boat Ramp
- Trail·Center
- Interpretive Center
- Shelter
- Equestrian Center
- ▲ Campground
- Group Camp
- Primitive Group Camp
- Trailer Sanitation Station
- P Parking
- Fishing Pier

Location

Sibley State Park is located in Kandiyohi County, 4 miles west of New London and 15 miles north of Willmar. The main entrance to the park is on County Road 48 off of US 71. This wooded hilly 2,300-acre park that bears the name of Minnesota's first governor, is located in an area where the grass-lands of the west meet the Big Woods of the east. Mt. Tom, which rises to an elevation of 1,375 feet above sea level, is the highest point for 50 miles. It affords an excellent view of surrounding forest, prairie knolls, lakes, and farmland.

Facilities & Activities

137 drive-in campsites
52 campsites with electricity
dump station
flush toilets (H)
vault toilets (H)
showers (H)
horse camping (50 capacity)
modern group camp (120 capacity)
rustic group camp (150 capacity)
picnic area with open shelter
swimming
fishing (lake)
boat launch
boat & canoe rental
visitor center (year-round)
interpretive program (year-round)
winter access
park store
motor rental
warming house
fishing pier
18 miles of foot trails
1 mile of self-guided trails
5 miles of horseback riding trails
5 miles of bike trails
10 miles of X-country ski trails
6 miles of snowmobile trails

REGION 3

Split Rock Creek State Recreation Area

For Information

Split Rock Creek State Recreation Area
Route 2
Jasper, MN 56144
(507) 348-7908

For centuries, the Dakotah Indians and other tribes used the pipestone from the quarry in this area to carve their ceremonial peace pipes. Pipe Stone National Monument, and this model Indian Village are nearby.

Location

Split Rock Creek State Recreation Area is located 6 miles south of Pipestone and 1 mile south of Ihlen on State Highway 23. Access to the area is from Pipestone County Road 20. Because Split Rock Lake is the only sizable body of water in Pipestone County, this 238-acre recreation area provides year-round recreation found nowhere else in the county and is a haven for waterfowl and other aquatic birds.

Facilities & Activities

28 drive-in campsites
14 campsites with electricity
flush toilets (H)
showers (H)
rustic group camp
picnic area with open shelter
swimming
fishing (lake)
boat launch
canoe rental
visitor center (year-round)
winter access
warming house
skating rink
2 miles of foot trails
2 miles of X-country ski trails

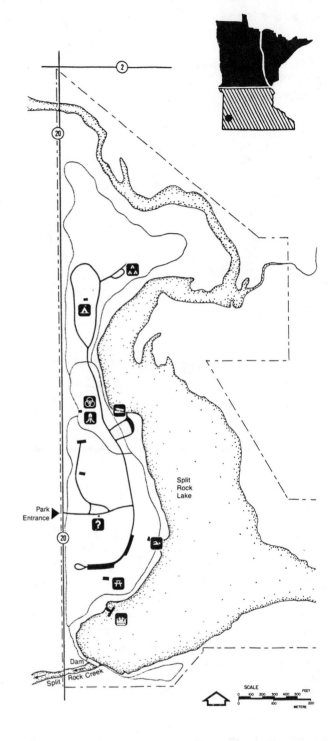

FACILITIES

? Information
⛩ Picnic Area
🏖 Beach
🚤 Boat Ramp
⛺ Campground

♦ Primitive Group Camp
⊕ Interpretive Center
🚶 Trail Center
🎣 Fishing Pier

TRAILS

------ Hiking

Upper Sioux Agency State Park

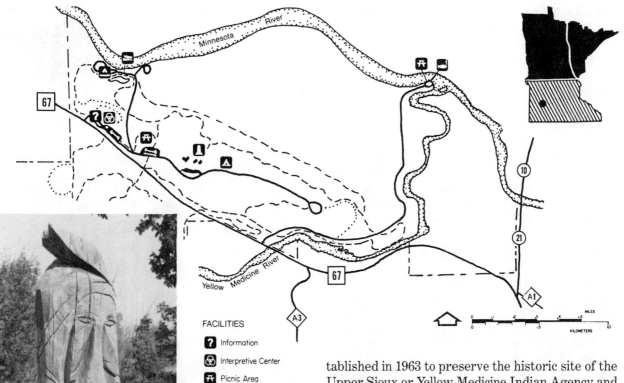

FACILITIES

?	Information
	Interpretive Center
	Picnic Area
	Historic Site (Upper Sioux Agency)
	Boat Ramp
	Fishing Access
	Campground
	Canoe Campground

TRAILS

·········· Hiking

– – – Horseback / Hiking

This impressive Sioux, hewn from a tree on the banks of the Minnesota River, greets you as you step from your canoe.

For Information

Upper Sioux Agency State Park
Rt. 2, Box 92
Granite Falls, MN 56241
(612) 564-4777

Location

Upper Sioux Agency State Park is located on State Highway 67, 8 miles southeast of Granite Falls in Yellow Medicine County. The park was es-tablished in 1963 to preserve the historic site of the Upper Sioux or Yellow Medicine Indian Agency and to provide recreational opportunities in the scenic Minnesota River Valley. For hundreds of years before the first white men explored the Minnesota River Valley, the Dakota (Sioux) people hunted, fished, and lived here. The park covers 1,066 acres of the southern bluffs of the Minnesota River and confluence with the Yellow Medicine River. In 1969, the historic site was given to the Minnesota Historical Society for research, preservation and development purposes.

Facilities & Activities

15 drive-in campsites
1 canoe campsite
vault toilets (H)
horse camping
picnic area with open shelter (H)
fishing (river)
boat launch
visitor center (seasonal)
winter access
historic site
8 miles of foot trails
1 mile of self-guided trails
12 miles of horseback riding trails
2 miles of X-country ski trails
9 miles of snowmobile trails

Whitewater State Park

For Information

Whitewater State Park
Rt. 1, Box 256
Altura, MN 55910
(507) 932-3007

Location

Whitewater State Park is located in Winona County on State Highway 74, 3 miles south of Elba and 9 miles north of St. Charles at I-90 exit 233. The river running through this 2,800-acre park got its name from the Indians because in the spring the river turned milky white as highwater eroded the light-colored clay deposits of its banks.

Many parks have hands-on activities as part of the interpretive program; most programs are seasonal, Whitewater's is year-round.

This impressive footbridge spans Whitewater River and gives a great view of the stream as well as the sandy beach and swimming area.

About the Park

The blufflands of southeastern Minnesota are well represented by Whitewater State Park with its dolomite cliffs, trout streams, and hardwood forests. Examples of the geology, plants, animals, and history typical of this part of the state can be found within the boundaries of the park, which has diverse recreational opportunities and a noticeable absence of mosquitoes.

Whitewater State Park has two interpretive facilities. The interpretive center located in Gooseberry Glen Campground includes a number of "hands on" displays relating to local plants, widlife, and history. The Chimney Rock Geological Center exhibits a slide show and displays on the geological history of southeastern Minnesota's Blufflands. These interpretive facilities are open daily during the summer and on weekends spring and fall.

Facilities & Activities

112 drive-in campsites
dump station
flush toilets (H)
vault toilets (H)
showers (H)
modern group camp (132 capacity)
rustic group camp (100 capacity)
2 picnic areas with an open shelter
swimming
fishing (stream)
2 interpretive centers (year-round)
interpretive program (year-round)
winter access
10 miles of foot trails
2.5 miles of self-guided trails
4 miles of X-country ski trails

Whitewater State Park *(continued)*

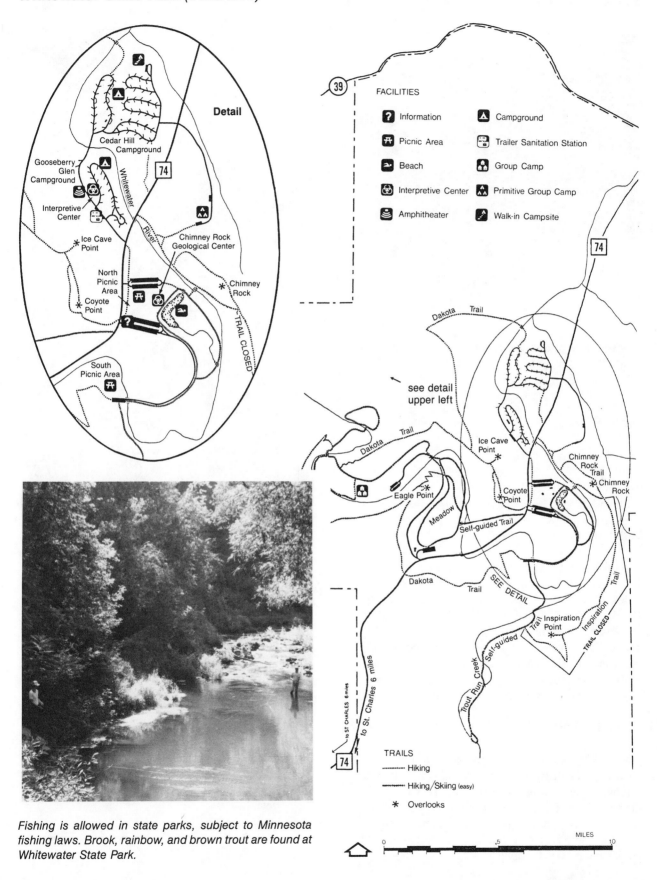

Detail

Cedar Hill Campground

Gooseberry Glen Campground

Interpretive Center

Ice Cave Point

North Picnic Area

Coyote Point

Chimney Rock Geological Center

Chimney Rock

South Picnic Area

Whitewater River

74

TRAIL CLOSED

FACILITIES

- **?** Information
- **Picnic Area**
- **Beach**
- **Interpretive Center**
- **Amphitheater**
- **Campground**
- **Trailer Sanitation Station**
- **Group Camp**
- **Primitive Group Camp**
- **Walk-in Campsite**

39

74

Dakota Trail

see detail upper left

Ice Cave Point

Chimney Rock Trail

Chimney Rock

Eagle Point

Coyote Point

Meadow

Self-guided Trail

Dakota Trail

SEE DETAIL

Inspiration Point

Inspiration Trail

TRAIL CLOSED

Self-guided

Trout Run Creek

to ST CHARLES 6 miles

to St. Charles 6 miles

74

TRAILS

- ········· Hiking
- ━━━━ Hiking/Skiing (easy)
- * Overlooks

MILES

0   .5   1.0

Fishing is allowed in state parks, subject to Minnesota fishing laws. Brook, rainbow, and brown trout are found at Whitewater State Park.

REGION 3

Wild River State Park

Sunrise Landing, and the park's main landing 10 miles downstream, are both located in the park, as are 15 canoe campsites.

For Information

Wild River State Park
Rt. 1, Box 75
Center City, MN 55012
(612) 583-2125

Location

Wild River State Park is located 13 miles east of I-35 at North Branch off State Highway 95, then 3 miles northeast of Almelund on Chisago County Road 12. The 7,000-acre park is one of the newest state parks in Minnesota, officially opening in 1978. The park's name "Wild River" is derived from the fact that the St. Croix River was one of the original 8 rivers protected by the U.S. Congress through the Wild and Scenic Rivers Act of 1968.

About the Park

Wild River State Park, established to protect the natural and cultural resources and to provide recreational opportunities along the St. Croix River, borders the river for approximately 20 miles. One popular canoe trip at the park is the 10-mile trip from the Sunrise River boat landing downstream to the park's main boat landing.

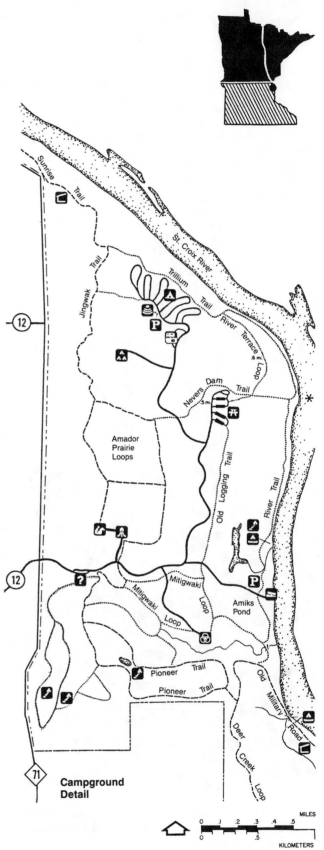

Campground Detail

Wild River State Park *(continued)*

Facilities & Activities

96 drive-in campsites
5 backpack campsites
15 canoe campsites
17 campsites with electricity
dump station
flush toilets (H)
vault toilets (H)
winterized showers (H)
horse camping (100 capacity)
rustic group camp (200 capacity)
2 picnic areas (H)
enclosed and open shelters
fishing (river)
2 boat launches
canoe rental
visitor center (year-round)
interpretive program (year-round)
outdoor amphitheater (300 capacity)

winter access
warming house
ski rental
canoe shuttle
historic site
35 miles of foot trails
1 mile of self-guided trails
20 miles of horseback riding trails
35 miles of X-country ski trails

The interpretive center, located on the bluff above the river, is a year-round facility with natural and historical displays. Park naturalists conduct programs throughout the year.

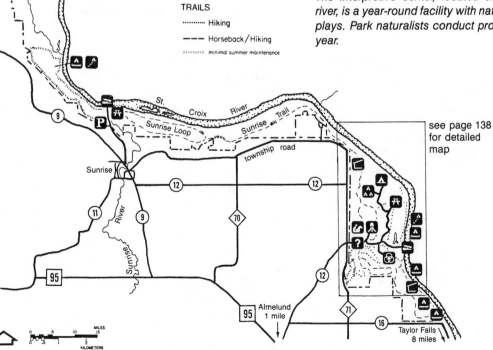

FACILITIES
? Information
Trail Center
Interpretive Center
P Parking Lot
Amphitheater
Picnic Area
Trail Shelter

Boat Landing
Campground
Primitive Group Camp
Walk-in Camping
Canoe Camping
Trailer Sanitation Station
Horse Camp

TRAILS
.... Hiking
--- Horseback/Hiking
.... minimal summer maintenance

see page 138 for detailed map

REGION 3

William O'Brien State Park

For Information

William O'Brien State Park
16821 O'Brien Trail North
Marine-on-St. Croix, MN 55047
(612) 433-2421

FACILITIES
- ? Information
- Trail/Interpretive Center
- Picnic Area
- Beach
- Boat Access
- Trail Shelter
- Campground
- Canoe Camping
- Group Camp
- Trailer Sanitation Station

TRAILS
- —— Bicycle/Hiking
- ········ Ski or Hiking

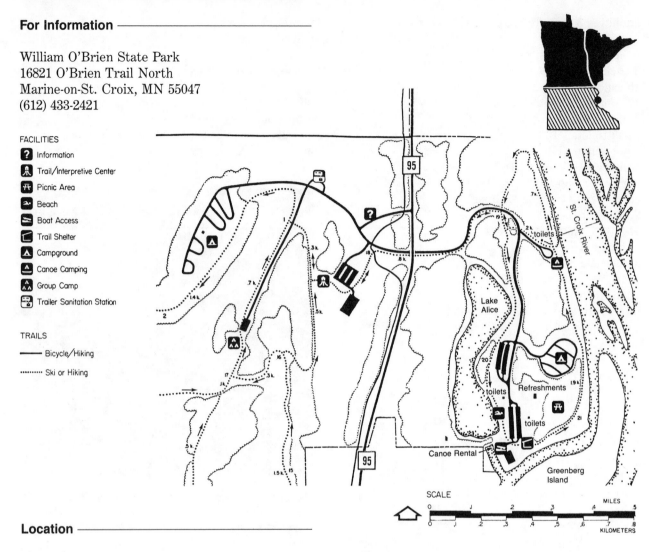

SCALE

MILES

KILOMETERS

Location

William O'Brien State Park is located on the St. Croix River in Washington County on Highway 95, 2 miles north of Marine-on-St. Croix. The scenic bluffs of the St. Croix River Valley help make canoeing a popular pastime. Canoes can be rented from within or outside the park from concessionaires by the day or hour. A shuttle service for cars and/or passengers is provided during the summer season from Taylor's Falls or Osceola.

Facilities & Activities

125 drive-in campsites at 2 campgrounds
1 group canoe campground (50 capacity)
62 campsites with electricity
dump station
flush toilets (H)
showers (H)
rustic group camp (75 capacity)
picnic area with 3 shelters (H)
swimming
fishing (river & lake)
boat launch
canoe rental
visitor center (year-round)
interpretive program (year-round)
winter access
warming house
ski rental
boat motor restrictions on Lake Alice
snack bar
canoe shuttle
9.5 miles of foot trails
1.5 miles of self-guided trails
2 miles of bike trails & access to county bike trail system
9.5 miles of X-country ski trails

Camping Equipment Checklist

The following checklists are designed to guide you in planning your next camping trip. Your needs will vary according to the type, length, and destination of your trip, as well as personal preferences, number of persons included, season of the year, and budget limitations.

Obviously, all items on the checklists aren't needed on any one trip. Since using checklists helps you think more methodically in planning, these extensive lists should serve merely as a reminder of items you may need.

When using these checklists to plan a trip, the item may be checked (✔) if it needs to be taken. Upon returning, if the item was considered unnecessary, a slash could be used: ✘. If a needed item was forgotten, a zero could be used (0); if the item has been depleted and needs to be replenished, an encircling of the check could be used; ⟲. This is of particular importance if you camp regularly and keep a camping box packed with staples that can be ready to go on a moment's notice.

Cooking equipment needs are quite dependent on the menu—whether you plan to cook and eat three balanced meals a day or whether you plan to eat non-cooked meals or snacks the entire trip. Many campers find it helpful to jot down the proposed menu for each meal on a 4" × 6" index card to help determine the grocery list as well as the equipment needed to prepare the meal. By planning this way, you'll avoid taking equipment you'll never use and you won't forget important items.

Typical Menu with Grocery and Equipment Needs

MEAL: Saturday breakfast		Number of Persons: 5
MENU	GROCERY LIST	EQUIPMENT
orange juice	Tang	camp stove
bacon	10 slices bacon	gasoline, funnel
eggs (scrambled)	8 eggs	folding oven
biscuits	1 can biscuits	frying pan
	peach jelly	baking pan
	honey	pitcher
	margarine	mixing bowl
	salt	cooking fork, spoon
	pepper	

Shelter/Sleeping:

___ Air mattresses
___ Air mattress pump
___ Cots, folding
___ Cot pads
___ Ground cloth
___ Hammock
___ Mosquito netting
___ Sleeping bag or bed roll
___ Tarps (plastic & canvas)
___ Tent
___ Tent stakes, poles, guy ropes
___ Tent repair kit
___ Whisk broom

Extra Comfort:

___ Camp stool
___ Catalytic heater
___ Folding chairs
___ Folding table
___ Fuel for lantern & heater
___ Funnel
___ Lantern
___ Mantels for lantern
___ Toilet, portable
___ Toilet chemicals
___ Toilet bags
___ Wash basin

Clothing/Personal Gear:

___ Bathing suit
___ Boots, hiking & rain
___ Cap/hat
___ Facial tissues
___ Flashlight (small), batteries
___ Jacket/windbreaker
___ Jeans/trousers
___ Pajamas

___ Pocket knife
___ Poncho
___ Prescription drugs
___ Rain suit
___ Sheath knife
___ Shirts
___ Shoes
___ Shorts
___ Socks
___ Sweat shirt/sweater
___ Thongs (for showering)
___ Toilet articles (comb, soap, shaving equipment, toothbrush, toothpaste, mirror, etc.)
___ Toilet paper
___ Towels
___ Underwear
___ Washcloth

Safety/Health:

___ First-aid kit
___ First-aid manual
___ Fire extinguisher
___ Insect bite remedy
___ Insect repellant
___ Insect spray/bomb
___ Poison ivy lotion
___ Safety pins
___ Sewing repair kit
___ Scissors
___ Snake bite kit
___ Sunburn lotion
___ Suntan cream
___ Water purifier

Optional:

___ Binoculars
___ Camera, film, tripod, light meter

___ Canteen
___ Compass
___ Fishing tackle
___ Frisbee, horseshoes, washers, etc.
___ Games for car travel & rainy day
___ Hobby equipment
___ Identification books: birds, flowers, rocks, stars, trees, etc.
___ Knapsack/day pack for hikes
___ Magnifying glass
___ Map of area
___ Notebook & pencil
___ Sunglasses

Miscellaneous:

___ Bucket/pail
___ Candles
___ Clothesline
___ Clothespins
___ Electrical extension cord
___ Flashlight (large), batteries
___ Hammer
___ Hand axe/hatchet
___ Nails
___ Newspapers
___ Pliers
___ Rope
___ Saw, bow or folding
___ Sharpening stone/file
___ Shovel
___ Tape, masking or plastic
___ Twine/cord
___ Wire
___ Work gloves

Cooking Equipment Checklist

**Food Preparation/
Serving/Storing:**

___ Aluminum foil
___ Bags (large & small,
    plastic & paper)
___ Bottle/juice can opener
___ Bowls, nested with lids for
    mixing, serving & storing
___ Can opener
___ Colander
___ Fork, long-handled
___ Ice chest
___ Ice pick
___ Knife, large
___ Knife, paring
___ Ladle for soups & stews
___ Measuring cup
___ Measuring spoon
___ Pancake turner
___ Potato & carrot peeler
___ Recipes
___ Rotary beater
___ Spatula
___ Spoon, large
___ Tongs
___ Towels, paper
___ Water jug
___ Wax paper/plastic wrap

Cooking:

___ Baking pans
___ Charcoal
___ Charcoal grill (hibachi or
    small collapsible type)
___ Charcoal lighter
___ Coffee pot
___ Cook kit, nested/pots &
    pans with lids
___ Fuel for stove (gas-
    oline/kerosene/liquid
    propane)
___ Griddle
___ Hot pads/asbestos gloves
___ Matches
    Ovens for baking:
___ Cast iron dutch oven
___ Folding oven for fuel
    stoves
___ Reflector oven
___ Tote oven
___ Skewers
___ Skillet with cover
___ Stove, portable
___ Toaster (folding camp
    type)
___ Wire grill for open fire

Eating:

___ Bowls for cereal, salad,
    soup
___ Cups, paper & styrofoam
___ Forks
___ Glasses, plastic
___ Knives
___ Napkins, paper
___ Pitcher, plastic
___ Plates (plastic, aluminum,
    paper)
___ Spoons
___ Table cloth, plastic
___ _____
___ _____

Clean-Up:

___ Detergent (Bio-degrad-
    able soap)
___ Dish pan
___ Dish rag
___ Dish towels
___ Scouring pad
___ Scouring powder
___ Sponge

Hiking/Backpacking Checklist

This list is not meant to be all inclusive or necessary for each trip. It is a guide in choosing the proper gear. Although this list was prepared for the hiker/backpacker, it is quite appropriate for anyone using the backcountry, whether they are traveling by foot, canoe, bicycle, or horse. Parentheses indicate those optional items that you may not want to carry depending upon the length of the trip, weather conditions, personal preferences, or necessity.

Ten Essentials for Any Trip:

___ Map
___ Compass
___ First-aid kit
___ Pocket knife
___ Signaling device
___ Extra clothing
___ Extra food
___ Small flashlight/extra
    bulb & batteries
___ Fire starter/candle/
    waterproof matches
___ Sunglasses

Day Trip (add to the above):

___ Comfortable boots or
    walking shoes
___ Rain parka or 60/40
    parka

___ Day pack
___ Water bottle/canteen
___ Cup
___ Water purification tablets
___ Insect repellant
___ Sun lotion
___ Chapstick
___ Food
___ Brimmed hat
___ (Guide book)
___ Toilet paper & trowel
___ (Camera & film)
___ (Binoculars)
___ (Book)
___ Wallet & I.D.
___ Car key & coins for
    phone
___ Moleskin for blisters
___ Whistle

Overnight or Longer Trips
(add the following):

___ Backpack
___ Sleeping bag
___ Foam pad
___ (Tent)
___ (Bivouac cover)
___ (Ground cloth/poncho)
___ Stove
___ Extra fuel
___ Cooking pot(s)
___ Pot scrubber
___ Spoon (knife & fork)
___ (Extra cup/bowl)
___ Extra socks
___ Extra shirt(s)
___ Extra pants/shorts
___ Extra underwear
___ Wool shirt/sweater
___ (Camp shoes)

___ Bandana
___ (Gloves)
___ (Extra water container)
___ Nylon cord
___ Extra matches
___ Soap
___ Toothbrush/powder/floss
___ Mirror
___ Medicines
___ (Snake bite kit)
___ (Notebook & pencil)
___ Licenses & permits
___ (Playing cards)
___ (Zip-lock bags)
___ (Rip stop repair tape)
___ Repair kit—wire, rivets,
    pins, buttons, thread,
    needle, boot strings

Index